ALLIES

REAL TALK
ABOUT
SHOWING UP,
SCREWING UP,
AND TRYING
AGAIN

ALLIES

EDITED BY
SHAKIRAH BOURNE
& DANA ALISON LEVY

First American Edition, 2021
Published in the United States by DK Publishing
1450 Broadway, Suite 801, New York, NY 10018

Page and cover design copyright © 2021 Dorling Kindersley Limited
DK, a Division of Penguin Random House LLC
21 22 23 24 25 10 9 8 7 6 5 4 3 2 1
002–324016–September/2021

"Dana's Absolutely Perfect Fail-Safe No Mistakes Guaranteed Way to Be an Ally"
Text copyright © Dana Alison Levy, 2021
"An Open Letter to the Young Black Queer" Text copyright © Cam Montgomery, 2021
"Hey Kid, Choose Your Battles" Text copyright © Eric Smith, 2021
"Round and Round We Go" Text copyright © Kayla Whaley, 2021
"This Is What It Feels Like" Text copyright © Andrew Sass, 2021
"A Bus, a Poster, and a Mirror" Text copyright © Brendan Kiely, 2021
"Travel Logs of a Black Caribbean Woman: Embracing the Glitches"
Text copyright © Shakirah Bourne, 2021
"Stutter Buddy" Text and Illustration copyright © Derick Brooks, 2021
"The Unsafe Space" Text copyright © Adiba Jaigirdar, 2021
"Dismantling Judgment" Text copyright © Lizzie Huxley-Jones, 2021
"Why Didn't Anyone Else Say Anything?" Text copyright © Naomi Evans and Natalie Evans, 2021
"From Author, to Ally, to Co-conspirator" Text copyright © Ilene Yi-Zhen Wong, 2021
"Lupe" Text copyright © Aida Salazar, 2021
"Did You Know Gandhi Was Racist?" Text copyright © Sharan Dhaliwal, 2021
"Lifting As She Climbs" Text copyright © Andrea L. Rogers, 2021
"Counting on Esteban" Text copyright © Marietta B. Zacker, 2021

This book is substantially a work of nonfiction based on the experiences and
recollections of the authors. In some cases names of people, places, dates, sequences,
or the detail of events have been changed to protect the privacy of others.

Jacket design by Anita Mangan

A catalog record for this book
is available from the Library of Congress.

ISBN 978-0-7440-3991-7

Printed and bound in Great Britain

For the curious
www.dk.com

To Marietta,
thanks for wearing all the hats.

To everyone reading,
thank you for taking this journey with us.

— Shakirah and Dana

WAIT!

We're so glad you're here, and we wanted to share some important information with you before you read on. Each of the personal essays in this book explores experiences about real things that happened to real people. Some of them cover topics that could make you feel anxious or upset. These experiences might remind you of things you've been through, or things that people you care about have been through. It's okay to put the book down, clear your head, and come back whenever you feel ready to read some more.

If you need support around any of the issues described in this book, check out the "*Stuff to think about, further reading, and more resources*" section at the back of the book where you can find out about some great organizations and get more information.

CONTENTS

DANA'S ABSOLUTELY PERFECT FAIL-SAFE NO MISTAKES GUARANTEED WAY TO BE AN ALLY

DANA ALISON LEVY

Hahahahaha! That's so . . . oh. Wait. You thought I was serious with that title?

Yeah, sorry about that.

Being a good ally without making mistakes is like eating popcorn without dropping any on the floor: it's possible, but let's be honest, it rarely happens.

For instance, let's try this quiz:

1. You (an able-bodied person) see someone in a wheelchair moving through a doorway. Should you:

   a. Rush to open the door for them

   b. Leave them alone

c. Ask them if they want help

   d. It's complicated

2. You (a white person) want to show support for a Black Lives Matter protest so you:

   a. Post on social media

   b. Attend a protest

   c. Write a letter to your local paper

   d. Do nothing: it's performative and you don't want to co-opt spaces for Black voices

   e. It's complicated

3. On social media an old friend you haven't talked to in years posts a cruel meme that disrespects transgender people. Creeping around her other posts, you see a lot of problematic content. Do you:

   a. Call her out and put her on blast

   b. Unfriend her

   c. Write a long passionate DM about why her stuff is a mess

   d. It's complicated

YOU GUESSED IT. BEING AN ALLY IS COMPLICATED. AND I CERTAINLY DON'T HAVE ALL THE ANSWERS. I HAVE SCREWED UP MORE TIMES THAN I CAN COUNT, AND IT FEELS GROSS EVERY TIME.

You guessed it. Being an ally is complicated. And I certainly don't have all the answers. I have screwed up more times than I can count, and it feels gross every time. I get nervous when I'm going to speak up or get involved, even after years of practice. But I still try.

But let's back up.

What do we even mean when we talk about being an ally? We can at least all agree on that, right?

Well, wrong, because there are lots of different ways of defining it and, more importantly, acting on that definition.

But here's a place to start.

> **BEING AN ALLY, FIRST OF ALL, IS A CONSTANT ACT—NOT A STATE OF BEING.**

Being an ally, first of all, is a constant act—not a state of being. You can be a wonderful ally in one situation and completely fail to act in another. It's not a level to reach in a game (Achievement unlocked! Level Ally! Upgrade your gems! That would be cool, but sadly, no). Being an ally is about someone other than yourself, and it's about supporting those others . . . whether or not you know them, whether or not they are aware you're supporting them, whether or not you have any personal connection.

One of the trickiest parts of being an ally is that no one is just one thing. The idea of intersectionality is where it really gets funky. Intersectionality means that no one is defined by just one element of themselves, and these different elements intersect and can even contradict.

So for instance: I am a woman, and I'm Jewish, two elements of my identity that, in our society, can elicit cruelty, ignorance, danger, and prejudice. However I am white, I am able-bodied, I'm middle class; all aspects of my identity that give me privilege. So in some situations I might be vulnerable, and in others, I have significantly more power than others in the room.

It's confusing, right?

If you're Black and wealthy and able-bodied; if you're white and queer and disabled; if you're Asian and visually impaired and female; if you're transgender and Latinx and famous . . . do you need an ally? Should you be showing up as an ally? Who "deserves" (and wow, there's a loaded word!) our allyship? Who can make the perfect judgment call to tell the rest of the world what's right and wrong?

Say it with me, loud for the folks in the back:

IT'S COMPLICATED.

It's even complicated to know what to call it. The term ally has become a common way to talk about the responsibilities we have to show up and support each other, and in particular for those with privilege to show up and support people and communities that are systemically oppressed. But not everyone thinks it's a great word. Some argue that too many people claim the label without doing the work. Others say it doesn't go far enough, and that allies might empathize with and support individuals, but they aren't doing the hard, sometimes dangerous work of breaking down oppressive systems. There are those who say we need accomplices, not allies, to really make change.

Did I mention it's complicated??

Here's one thing I know: these are good, important conversations about labels and what they mean. But we should not let the complexity of the word distract us from the urgency of the work. Whatever we call ourselves—an ally, an accomplice, a

WHATEVER WE CALL OURSELVES—AN ALLY, AN ACCOMPLICE, A CO-CONSPIRATOR—WE MUST DO BETTER TO UNDERSTAND, EMPATHIZE, AND TAKE ACTION TO CARE FOR EACH OTHER.

co-conspirator—we must do better to understand, empathize, and take action to care for each other.

Being an ally is not about your personal growth (though that's likely going to happen), or about diversifying your friendships (though that will likely happen, too). It's not about having all the answers to school those non-allies in everything they're doing wrong. Being an ally means that when you screw up (and you will), you apologize and do better . . . but you don't insist on forgiveness, or try to make the other person process it with you, or beat yourself up so badly that it suddenly becomes their job to reassure you!

So what is it? What is allyship?

It's continuously showing up and using the power you have— by speaking out, by physically using your body, by educating yourself, by using your resources (financial and otherwise), and by amplifying marginalized voices—in support of those who have less power due to ongoing systemic racism, ableism, sexism, religious persecution, and other forms of oppression.

There are a lot of definitions of being an ally, but one of my favorites comes from Dr. Laura Jiménez, an educator and advocate. On her *BookToss* blog, she has a shirt that reads: "ALLY: [noun/verb] To cause a ruckus and pass the mic."

I LOVE THIS DEFINITION.

Because as an ally, sometimes you have to make some noise, and sometimes you have to get out of the way and let others speak for themselves. And figuring out when to act and when to stay quiet is a constant learning process.

Allyship looks different depending on who you are and what stage of life you're in. An adult has different tools available than a teen. A celebrity with ten million social media followers has different tools than a college student. A bazillionaire philanthropist has different tools than me. But we all have power. And a dozen times a day we make decisions, large and small, on how we will use it.

The way we use our power depends on our strengths, our tools, and our comfort level. I'm going to talk about some of the quieter ways we can be allies . . . not because I don't think that sometimes we need to raise a ruckus, but because I'm better at the quiet stuff. I'm still working my way up to ruckus status.

So let's talk about some of the tools.

QUIET ALLYSHIP

Being an ally sometimes means quietly changing your habits in ways that others may never notice. Like what? You ask. How about:

- ▶ Buy your stuff—books, shoes, coffee, cupcakes—from BIPOC-owned businesses, locally or online

- ▶ Read books by diverse authors, and then hype them up to your friends

- ▶ Follow diverse voices on social media, especially local ones and folks without millions of followers. Amplify them and help them get noticed

- ▶ Educate yourself. Which Indigenous peoples might

have lived on the land where you live now? What other versions of history offer different perspectives than what you're reading in school?

► Share your pronouns, and normalize asking or being asked, so that gender fluid, non-binary, and transgender folks don't have the full burden of educating people

These are all ways of being an ally that don't require a lot of bravery or practice, and again, it's not something you'll do for a while then move on to Stage Two. This is lifelong work . . . we vote with our wallets and our time way more often than we ever get to vote in elections, so get in the habit of practicing allyship in small ways every day!

For me this means that when I give books as gifts—and I give a lot of books! It's kind of my thing—I almost always give books by diverse authors, usually focusing on new writers or those whose

> **THIS IS LIFELONG WORK . . . WE VOTE WITH OUR WALLETS AND OUR TIME WAY MORE OFTEN THAN WE EVER GET TO VOTE IN ELECTIONS, SO GET IN THE HABIT OF PRACTICING ALLYSHIP IN SMALL WAYS EVERY DAY!**

books aren't huge bestsellers. It means that I pay attention to a lot of incredibly smart people on social media who don't follow me back and never will, because I'm grateful to absorb their wisdom. It means I read more nonfiction than I used to, trying to fill the gaps in my knowledge left by a white supremacist education system.

And being a quiet ally also sometimes means just that—keeping quiet.

Remember when I said that it's not about you? Yeah, it's really not about you.

You, my dear ally-in-training, are going to be learning and processing and unlearning all through this journey! It's hard and it's tiring, and you definitely need friends to talk to. You might need a sympathetic shoulder to lean on. There might be a time you did something you're proud of, and you want to talk about it. You may even complain about how you tried to do the right thing but it backfired. Totally fair!

HOWEVER.

Do not drop that load of learning and missteps on the people you are trying to support! And that includes your friends! If you have a wonderful circle of diverse friends and you tried to be an ally and screwed up (Again! It's gonna happen. Get comfortable with it), the person to go to for tea and sympathy and a debrief is NOT your Black Friend or your Muslim Friend or your Disabled Friend or whatever friend of the same marginalization as the one you were defending. They are aware of the cruelty directed toward their communities—they don't need you to tell them all about it.

Part of the work of being an ally is taking that processing elsewhere, and sparing them the burden of your questions and guilt.

Yet another way of being a quiet ally is recognizing that sometimes you need to step back. Let's say you, a white person

> **BEING A GOOD ALLY OFTEN MEANS *NOT* SPEAKING UP WHEN THERE ARE FOLKS WHO CAN SPEAK FOR THEMSELVES.**

and ally, are at a local Black Lives Matter protest, and the newspaper reporter comes over to ask you about it. All around you are other protesters, many of whom are Black. Do you talk to the reporter, share all your outrage, and drop some hard facts around police violence? Or do you step away and urge them to talk to one of the Black protesters?

Like that quiz in the beginning . . . it's complicated. (For example, not everyone wants to be quoted in the newspaper; not everyone feels safe). But being a good ally often means NOT speaking up when there are folks who can speak for themselves.

I have had to consider this kind of allyship a lot lately. I'm a white woman who writes books for kids. There are a lot of us. There are a rather embarrassing number more white authors than BIPOC authors. And far too often at multi-author events, at conferences, book festivals, bookstores, and so on, I would sit with five or six other authors, and we were all white.

Not acceptable.

So I, and many others, made a pledge a few years ago: no more all-white panels. No more all-white conferences. No more token author of color amidst a sea of whiteness.

What that means is that when I get invited to a book event—and let me just say, it's not like they're beating down the door! I don't get a lot of these invitations, and it's always exciting when I do—but when I get invited, I ask the awkward question. I send an email thanking them, then say "I have taken a pledge to no longer participate in all-white book events. Can you tell me who else is invited and what other authors have committed to being there?" Or I might say "Thank you for inviting me to be on this panel. I've taken a pledge not to participate in all-white book events, so can I suggest you ask XX or YY to join instead?"

I often wind up declining the event. Sometimes the event organizers tell me they've invited certain BIPOC authors, but those authors declined. Sometimes they give a metaphorical shrug, like they did the best they could. Sometimes they're genuinely horrified when they realize their bias and are grateful for the insight. They promise to do better the following year. And often they do improve . . . but they don't always invite me back.

And I get it—the organizers are often volunteers, the events are often poorly paid, and like I said, there are way more white authors than BIPOC authors.

But it's not good enough. So I won't go. And I don't get cookies, and I don't get thanked, and if I'm being totally honest, I don't even get a glow of satisfaction. Sometimes I have FOMO and wish I had done the damn event, because I'm human and don't like missing out. And I'm not telling you now so YOU can give me cookies or tell me what a wonderful ally I am!

I'm sharing it because how can we know how to help if no one shows us? How can we use our power until someone points out that we have some?

Here's one final thought on being a quiet ally: consider calling in people in your circles who are using problematic language or sharing misinformation. Unless you live under a rock (and if you do, is it warm and cozy and can I join you?), you have probably heard about "Call-Out Culture" and "Cancel Culture." There is a tension between people being held accountable for their choices, and a kind of feeding frenzy of disapproval that can make the punishment outweigh the crime. This is a whole complicated mess of a subject, and it would take another essay

and several packages of cookies for me to even attempt to unpack it. But in short, it's the idea that the only way to get people to change is to publicly shame them.

And let me be clear: sometimes people need to be called out. Sometimes people with a lot of power—politicians, celebrities, even famous authors—say things that are unacceptably racist or prejudiced. And sometimes they do not step back when someone tries to explain the problem, but instead double down on their misbelief. And yes, in these cases, calling them out and holding them accountable, and seeking to educate the general public about their views, is justified and necessary.

But calling in is also a useful tool, and often can be tried before trying to shame someone into enlightenment. Calling in is when someone genuinely might not know that their statements are hurtful. Calling in offers someone a bridge back from their mistake, and is done with an assumption of good faith. It's saying: "You might not have known this, so I am telling you. And now that you know, you can do better."

Calling in is one way to be an ally, to make it clear that certain language or behavior isn't okay, without going to the nuclear option of publicly shaming someone. Here's an example: until fairly recently I did not realize there was anything problematic about the phrase "spirit animal." I had heard it used as a pop culture reference ("Taylor Swift is my spirit animal; Narwhals are my spirit animal") and thought it was clever and kind of funny.

Until I read how, as a very real part of Native American Indigenous traditions, this co-opting and joking version is totally disrespectful.

But it's just a joke, right?

But no one was trying to be offensive, right?

CALLING IN OFFERS SOMEONE A BRIDGE BACK FROM THEIR MISTAKE, AND IS DONE WITH AN ASSUMPTION OF GOOD FAITH. IT'S SAYING: "YOU MIGHT NOT HAVE KNOWN THIS, SO I AM TELLING YOU. AND NOW THAT YOU KNOW, YOU CAN DO BETTER."

But obviously we aren't serious, right?

Yeah. Wrong.

So now I have this knowledge, and I have it because I've read several different Native American authors' views on the subject. And yet people I know, who are generally aware and careful and—yes, good allies—are still using this phrase.

So I call them in. I don't retweet them or tag them in a social media post shaming them for the problematic language. I send a private message, saying "hey, this is something I learned recently, and here's a link to learn more, but the phrase 'spirit animal' is really problematic and you might want to change it."

I call people in a lot. Depending on the issue and how well I know them, it might be really uncomfortable or no big deal. I will not tell you how long I spend crafting a three-sentence private message sometimes, because it's embarrassing and probably explains why I keep missing work deadlines. But often when I take the time to do this, people are grateful.

Of course, not always. Remember earlier, when I talked about all us white authors flooding events? After I had signed the pledge, I reached out to another (white woman) author friend. I explained why I wasn't going to an upcoming event, and asked her if she would also commit to the pledge: if she would refuse to attend all-white author events.

She refused.

HOW CAN I BE SURE I HAVEN'T SCREWED THIS UP??

I explained my reasoning, shared the importance of representation, and offered up some statistics on publishing.* She still refused, saying she understood the issue but she had to think of her own book sales, and wasn't willing to miss out on opportunities in this way.

And that was the end of it. I didn't call her out. I didn't put her on blast. But I quietly changed my own calculus about whether I'd promote her books or give them as gifts or invite her to events. It wasn't a situation where I had a lot of power, but I used what I had.

And that's really what being a quiet ally means. It means recognizing the small bits of power everyone has—to buy things, to listen to things, to talk about things with friends and family— and being intentional in how we use them. You can probably think of ten more examples. You might be doing them right now. AWESOME. Keep doing them. You don't get a prize, or a cookie, but that doesn't mean it's not vitally important.

I'll be honest: writing this essay is really hard. I am balancing on a skinny ledge, arms pinwheeling frantically, hoping I don't fall down on either side. I don't feel like I know nearly enough to tell anyone else how to be an ally: SLAM! I fall over on the Impostor Syndrome side. I don't want to brag and claim space that others should have: CRASH! I fall the other way on the Centering Myself side. How can I be sure I haven't screwed this up??

That one's easy. I can't. I can't be sure. I might screw this up.

But I still have to try.

Am I raising a ruckus? Maybe not. Am I going to keep showing up, as best I can?

You'd better believe it.

Last quiz question:

4. You want to be an ally but you're afraid you don't know enough and you'll screw up. Should you:

    a. Read books and blogs, listen to podcasts, and follow activists and advocates on social media?

    b. Speak up to friends, family, classmates, and others when you hear something racist or oppressive?

    c. Find friends who are not part of marginalized groups who can support you while you figure out this ally stuff?

    d. Examine your own mistakes and learn from them but don't beat yourself up?

    e. It's complicated, but yeah, all of the above?

You know the answer, and so do I. So let's get back to work.

---

*Quick synopsis of the publishing statistics: they're dismal and almost all published kids' books are written by white authors. For more specifics, look at the Center for Diversity in Children's Literature's study.

AN OPEN LETTER TO THE YOUNG BLACK QUEER

CAM MONTGOMERY

Dear You,

My name is Cam. It used to be "Candice" but that person was never me. That person was gendered and named without her permission. That person was named by her brother—just five years her senior—and, you know what? It was the smallest amount of power that has ever gone to someone's head. And though the power in that responsibility was small, the weight of a name is always great.

So I lived as a Candice for a time. I was Candy as a kid. "Miss C" which became "Missy" as a young ballerina, all of age twelve. And in high school, Candice just sort of . . . settled and I lived with it. Uncomfortably.

Every time my parents used it, whether it was in disappointment, or as a simple request or acknowledgment—it always felt uncomfortable. At family cookouts in the deepest parts of South LA, my family used it to reintroduce me to people who had held me just that one time when I was a baby.

"You remember me?"

No, I never could remember those people. But apparently they knew me.

They knew Candice when I wanted to be Cam.

Cam.

Candice.

Amanda.

Montgomery.

That's my government name. But Cam is the one I've felt in my heart for as long as I can remember. It's the name that I felt should take precedence which, ironically, happened right around the time I started to notice my attraction to the opposite sex. Funny how that works, innit.

I was thirteen. Knobby, ashy knees, cuspate elbows and wrists. And at that time I was still Candice and that girl was enrolled in a private Baptist Christian high school where we prayed before every class—twice during Bible class—and the answer to sex education was "We don't do that here!"

So, all the answers I sought were nowhere to be found. Not at school where maybe one or two of my peers might have been able to commiserate. Not at home or hanging out with my cousins where my traditional, binary Black family never used the words "gay" or "queer" except maybe as insults when playing the dozens.

I didn't knowingly meet any queer people IRL until I made it to college at age eighteen.

I didn't realize being queer was an option for me. I didn't realize that my sexual preferences, who I chose to love, my gender, my personal presentation, and my choice in pronouns were all pliable, living on a very long scale. I had options insofar as how those pieces of me would fit. It was my decision.

Unreal, right? I didn't realize any of this could be for me—not until I took my first Gay Male Writers course two years later. That class is where my favorite undergraduate professor, one Dr. Martin Pousson, introduced himself to the class as "Out™ and outrageously homosexual." He stressed the fact that we were not to call him "Mr. Pousson" because "that's my father's name and my name is Martin, sugar." And then he proceeded to play "Let's Have a Kiki" by Scissor Sisters.

Iconiccccc.

I'd taken a class or two with him in previous semesters but this was the 300-level class where he gave us the option to introduce ourselves by name, pronoun, and/or orientation.

And wouldn't you know it, I was one of the last to go. Which gave me time to Google all the pronouns and orientations I didn't know/had never in my life heard of.

Oh, that sweet summer child.

I still think back on that day sometimes. It was over ten years ago. I remember what I was wearing, how sweaty my back was getting. I remember the sensation of my heartbeat taking up residence in my stomach.

My knowledge was limited. Incredibly stunted, which—even had I not been a giant queer—would have been a disservice to me. Because it limited my world view. It put a lid on the scope of my thinking and my entire scope of the world.

I was a bird with a bad wing until that day when I heard a girl—she was maybe the fifth or sixth person to introduce herself—say she was pansexual.

Pansexual.

Hearing it was one thing. Understanding it was like coming home.

I typed in the term fast with my Johnson's Baby Lotion-slippery fingers, palms sweaty, phone hidden beneath the desk.

The Google search asked, Feeling Lucky? And, for one heartbreaking moment, wallahi, I was.

I hit search.

My world opened up its mouth wide, swallowed me whole.

Everything clicked. Everything, all of it.

All of the attraction I'd felt for women in media (shout out to Michiru and Haruka on *Sailor Moon*—the non-cousins), on campus, in my ballet company, made so much sense then.

The very definition of the term "pansexual" is what then helped me realize all the ridiculousness of the gender binary.

Pansexual, on occasion, gets tossed in with "bisexual." And though the two are similar, they are not the same. They simply share space.

MY WORLD OPENED UP ITS MOUTH WIDE, SWALLOWED ME WHOLE.

EVERYTHING CLICKED. EVERYTHING, ALL OF IT.

Bisexual is the attraction to two or more genders. Meaning multiple. And not necessarily male and female exclusively. There are many genders and this all includes those who ID as non-binary, meaning neither male nor female. So, bisexuality simply means the choice of two or more.

Pansexuality swings a little differently. Pansexual means that I share an attraction to any and all genders.

The difference?

Multiple is not the same as all.

That same day, when I grabbed "Pansexual" as a label and said "this is mine now" was the same day I discovered non-binary as an option for me, too.

I was supposed to go to work after that class and I didn't. I couldn't. I called out sick and spent the rest of the afternoon in my rented room searching for pieces of myself on the Internet.

My dearest friend, stand-in mother figure, and closest confidante at the time was my direct supervisor, Roxy. A forty-something, self-described hardcore Bolivian lady who enjoyed her office, coffee, and humor dark. She was the first person I came out to. I did it the next day, actually. Walked into my on-campus office job, straight into her office. I threw my body down onto her couch and unloaded. She wasn't familiar with any of the new things I'd learned only yesterday either, but she took them all in stride. She was so . . . just, happy. It blew my mind to see her react to me and all my excited confusion like that.

In a way, I was luckier than most. Because I know and understand that not everyone's first experience with coming out goes over that well. It certainly shouldn't be that way. But it is. And you and I and many of our friends, I know, are working to fix that.

Over the years, my label has changed and morphed. I went from cis hetero to cis pansexual to cis demisexual panromantic to "sis, we are non-binary demisexual panromantic! You may call us Cam now."

But there was a lot to be done before I got there . . . a lot of different reactions I had.

First was my reaction to learning the term "body dysmorphia."

Body dysmorphia is the perception of your body/the image of your body being "off" or "bad" or "wrong," which begets the thinking that you need to fix it, need to hide it. It's actually so much deeper than that, but there's the gist of it.

How long had I been struggling with this? How long had I been quietly dying inside my own skin. There was so much to unpack.

There was first the issue of me being a dark-skinned Black girl. We're disrespected enough as is. But add to that the fact that I didn't even know I was trying to hide more than my dark skin and my 4C kinky curls—what a revelation!

Some of those revelations made more sense when I thought about my closet full of baggy sweaters, the way I wore just enough makeup to lighten my skin but not make me appear overly feminine, and my preference to let Vicky keep her secret so long as I could keep my sports bras.

I was angry. Angry that I'd been kept in the dark for so long. Angry that I was never given the chance to talk about or explore these things as possibilities.

Los Angeles is not a conservative city. It never has been, not even at the beginning of the 21st century! But still, somehow, I was one of many, many Black kids raised in a family that did not speak of such things. I was raised in a family where, if the term "gay" did ever come up as something other than an insult, it was used in reference to "that uncle we don't associate with anymore."

The very furthest end of that discussion stopped at the LG portion of LGBTQ. None of the other letters existed in any kind of discussion.

The Black community has, historically, been very homophobic. There has been little understanding in our communities. Now, I'm extremely pleased to say that I've seen—have witnessed—some turnaround. Not just with my family but with other Black families, too. There are times when I've hit an elementary or high school to talk about books and the kids that show up are of the A-team. The Black Queers show up and show out.

We are made of something golden.

You are made of something golden.

I've said all this to point out the fact that, dear closeted Black queer—I was you, ma fleur. I was in the dark, and not of my own volition. I was lost and stumbled my way through all of it.

But at the same time, there are resources now that help people like us. People who don't have friends or family members who are willing to open up that bright-ass rainbow door and walk through it with us.

My professor, Dr. Martin Pousson, was this bass baritone-voiced gay white man from some Acadian city in Louisiana. He was my doorway to all things queer.

But I walked through it with friends I made along the way. A lot of them Black.

Which is almost comical, I'd say? Because Martin was a fifty-something white man living in Los Angeles, California. A white gay man who was born and raised in the deep and dirty south of Louisiana.

I think that's why we connected as quickly as we did, though.

My family's from the NOLA. His family was a few hours away from the big city, but it was a shared commonality. For us to share pieces of our Southern selves with one another. From there, I know a bond was built. Brick by brick, slow and steady. But as the trust was there, so, too, was that doorway I mentioned.

ONE THING I FIND MYSELF WISHING QUITE OFTEN IS THAT THERE WAS AT LEAST ONE PERSON WHO JUMPED OUT AT ME AS SOON AS I CROSSED THAT DOORWAY'S THRESHOLD AND SAID, "HEY. I'M HERE, TOO. LET'S DO THIS THING TOGETHER."

One thing I find myself wishing quite often is that there was at least one person who jumped out at me as soon as I crossed that doorway's threshold and said, "Hey. I'm here, too. Let's do this thing together."

Because even though I had made it to that door with some grace and then went through it, there was still a helluva lot of loneliness within my struggle.

I made it. Of course, I made it. I had help, though. And that's what I'm here trying to tell you, to show you.

My quiet Black queer, you absolute rose of a human—I am here for you. With you. I'm an author who writes books for you. With you and only you in mind. I speak out and I wake up and leave my house and smile and tell jokes on the Internet and do school visits because you, my friend, keep me going.

I'm here for you.

I am working and pushing and learning and being inspired by you.

And I'm here for you.

I am checking in with myself, with my biases, with my internalized this-and-that-or-another and I. Am. Here. For. You.

You may not know me. Not before now. And that's totally okay, my dude. But you do now. And I invite you to seek me out, to find me. Or maybe not; maybe it just helps you to know that there is someone—at least one someone who has your back 100%, undeniably and unconditionally.

I'm here for you. Full stop. And I know I wouldn't be the only one. There are resources like Black Trans Femmes In the Arts, The

IT IS MY SINCEREST WISH
THAT BLACK QUEERS
NEVER HAVE TO BE THAT
LOST IN THEIR OWN SKIN
EVER AGAIN.

LGBTQ+ Freedom Fund, Brave Space Alliance, and The Audre Lord Project out there now that are keyed in for us.

It is my sincerest wish that Black queers never have to be that lost in their own skin ever again. I find it wholly unacceptable that any queer person should have to wait until the age of twenty-one to "allow" themselves a label that they've feverishly Googled for five minutes.

A year or so ago, my cousin (he's twenty-five now) came out to me as bisexual. The entire family has long teased him about being "too sensitive," etc., and it's been no secret that I've been open and out for a decade now. But before that, while I remained quiet/questioning, he remained himself. Not labeled or out—just himself. And for being himself, he was pushed down and held under society's heteronormative thumb. He was told time and again, "That's not what a strong Black man does. That's not how we act."

And even though he never openly admitted it, I still felt . . . inordinately proud of him. He told me once, "I don't know what they're talking about, cuzzo. I'm not doing anything. I'm just sitting here doing me."

And, like . . . hello! OKAY, TRUTH! PROUDDDD!!!

To be so inside of you that you cannot fathom any other way to be. I still haven't admitted any of this to him. He was being picked apart for being """"soft"""" before I was vocal about who I was myself.

But just before he got real with me, that cousin told me he'd never felt closer to any person than he did when I started getting busy being obnoxious and loud about my Blackness and the ways it holds hands with my queerness.

I make no claims about being some kind of revolutionary. Jesus, it took me a good bit of time to even admit I could be—had permission from no one but me and myself to be—queer.

But if being loud and open and in your face about my queerness as a Black person makes any kind of difference for you, if it opens a door for you to step through and proceed unbothered, then I am thrilled and happy to claim that job.

It wasn't always my goal to be this person. To be the loud one who tries to make it okay for other Black queer kids to be loud and happy and full of vibrant, jumping color. But . . . "oops" in one hand, total and complete chaos in the other. See what you've got more of.

So here we are.

And here I am. Loud and proud and hoping it helps you.

Sometimes, being loud about my Blackness, my queerness, is simply for my own kind of release. And I've come to find that expression beautiful. Sometimes I'm loud about who I am because it's my passion. Because I must. Because nothing feels right or real unless or until I've declared it out loud with a full audience, be it a friend or a group of teens in a class I'm teaching or all my conservative relatives on the Facebook.

It should be okay for us to feel that way. Proud and proud to be loud. It's not always so and many of you—I am so sorry—know that all too well, up close, personal, and unavoidable.

It should be okay for us to be prideful and not worry about the roof over our heads, having food in our bellies, being nourished in the soul-deep way a family is meant to give.

So this is for you, my budding flowers with so much potential.

This is for you if you bleed in rainbow technicolor. This is for you if those thoughts you're holding in have started to burn. This is for you if you've ever pulled off to the side of the road to capture a single breath before all the rest of your heartbeats turn still and silent in your chest as you once again must hold yourself in at home. This is for you if you feel there isn't a single thing else you can do now.

This is for you, young blood, if you're reading this and think it is for you.

Love, your forever-ally,

Cam

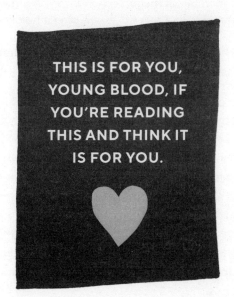

HEY KID, CHOOSE YOUR BATTLES

ERIC SMITH

For most of my peers growing up, junior high was a time of major firsts. The sort of firsts you carry with you your whole life and which form the frame of the picture of who you grow up to be. First crushes, first kisses, first heartbreaks . . .

Me? It was the first time I fought back, thanks to friends who explained what it was I was fighting.

As a kid, a lot of my young life was this fraught search for answers surrounding the why of the bullies in my life. In fact, my adult life sometimes zeroes in on that, late at night, randomly looking them up on Facebook. I find myself wondering, how did they turn out? Did they change? How did life turn out for them? It didn't make much sense to me, getting kicked around by other kids who, for the most part, didn't seem all that different from me. They ran in groups that were adjacent to my own and were often at parties with friends of mine. And since this was the mid-90s, those parties did usually involve Rollerblades or public ice-skating rinks.

It was a time full of puzzlement and awkward self-discovery, building on top of events that left me with so many questions. Like, why did people laugh so hard when I brought in Irish soda bread for "share a food from your culture day" in grade school? Why did some kids I barely knew think it was okay to ask why I didn't look like my family? And why was it so important to them that I knew where I was from, to the point that it went from giggles to abject violence over the course of a few years?

So, what does it mean to be a transracial adoptee? It depends on who you ask, and what their

I WAS A BOOK WITH A TITLE THAT DIDN'T FIT THE STORY.

lived experience is. No one person's experience is a monolith for everyone else, as they say. But for me, being a Latinx / Middle Eastern kid adopted by a white family, brought these challenges, of being raised without the culture I was "supposed" to have. I was unusual to other people.

And unfortunately, kids fear what they don't understand. And sometimes attack it.

When I was around thirteen or so, that's when I started really owning the fact that I was an adoptee. Started bringing it up with friends more, not holding onto it like it was some secret that needed to be kept. I had started to realize that if I just talked about it more, it helped avoid confusion. It got it out of the way, like ripping off a bandage. I looked like a Middle Eastern or Latinx kid, but unlike a vast majority of my friends, I didn't speak any other languages. My name promised someone different. I was a book with a title that didn't fit the story.

So, what do being adopted and being bullied by racists have to do with one another?

When you're a transracial adoptee raised in a bubble where racism isn't discussed or explained to you, so very much.

There are a lot of memories that bubble to the surface when I think about the hard time I had. The kid who knocked me down on the playground so hard that my saxophone snapped out of its hard-shell case and skidded across concrete. The kids who stole my jacket in one of the harshest winters we'd had, passing it up and down the unheated school bus. But the day I fought back against [Redacted] is the one memory that comes screaming back every single time.

And despite the urge to name these kids, I'll resist.

When you're younger, there's this burning desire to promise yourself that one day, you'll get back at those who wronged you. Even as a writer, you joke that you'll name people after the folks that caused you pain. But as the years pass, so does that want.

It's called growth, and I want that for you.

I don't remember what the cracks were in the hallway that particular day. The jokes. I ignored them, as I often did, hurrying by with my head down whenever I saw any of the kids who liked to pick on me, usually gathering together near their lockers. But then [Redacted] said the phrase that shook me.

"And at least I have real parents."

And I snapped. Everyone has their breaking point, and for me, it was always that strange insult of saying my parents aren't real. They're not imaginary. That's not how adoption works. They aren't some figment of my fever dream imagination. It's a go-to jab of the ignorant, and as a kid I couldn't stand it.

I screamed something at him and shoved him. And he proceeded to push me back, through the hallway doors leading to the staircase, and tossed me down the steps. He stomped angrily by me, yelling something else at me on the floor, about how I'd better never stand up to him again. He left me on the landing, thankfully unhurt save for some harsh bruises that would purple my arms and legs in the coming days, as well as my confidence.

But his best friend, [Redacted #2], stopped and helped me up.

"Hey, you've got to choose your battles," [Redacted #2] said, before shaking his head and walking off, to the school bus that we would all take together back to our neighborhood, sitting just mere feet away from one another, acting as though these acts of physical and emotional violence weren't even a thing. Where we'd all wait for the bus the next morning, together. Every. Single. Arduous. Day.

I think about that kid a lot. Not the one who pushed me down the stairs, but the one who helped me up. [Redacted #2]. The fourteen-year-old with the gravitas of a character in a True Detective story, insisting I was in the wrong fight. Like some kind of a grizzled police chief near retirement.

People will often tell you to choose your battles. To know when it's time to fight, and time to run. What moments you should use your voice, and what moments you should opt to stay quiet. But here's the thing. It can feel impossible to choose your battles when you have no idea what people are fighting with you about. When other people are the ones battling you. This moment felt different, this time. Maybe it was the degree of violence involved, being thrown down a staircase while other students hurried by, not wanting to get involved. Maybe it was the one kid, [Redacted #2], who gave me his hand and offered an attempt at advice.

But when I got home and turned to my neighborhood friends to talk about what had been happening and the things that were being said, it felt like this big breakthrough. I talked about how these other kids were insulting my family, bringing up the way I looked. How they talked about the color of my skin. And that I didn't understand why.

And it wasn't just at school. It all came pouring out.

How the trend had continued during my time in the Boy Scouts, with neighborhood kids who knew those other kids from my school. Where, under the supposed protection of other grownups, I got called a string of names that I couldn't grasp that everyone else thought was funny. And when I turned to the adults, the people who ran the Boy Scout troop, there wasn't an answer. No accountability. Just lots of squirming and uncomfortable looks between one another.

It was the first time I heard someone say, "well, boys will be boys" as though that was an acceptable excuse for horrible behavior. Please note, it isn't.

There was this church my friends and I used to hang outside of, across the street from a corner store that sold candy, soda, and plenty of junk food that we'd spend our meager allowances on. And it was there, sitting on top of a brick wall overlooking a busy sidewalk and busier street, that one of my friends shook her head, looked at me, and said "damn, that's racist."

But I didn't understand it. Not yet.

I didn't know it at the time, but I hadn't quite gotten a grip on what racism was, because I'd been raised in a bubble as a transracially adopted kid. There weren't any adults in my life who were willing, or able, to sit down and teach me what it was that was happening to me. To be that ally who sat me down and said this is how the world is, and here's how you can navigate it, and some ways that I'll help you. That these bullies in your life have a reason for why they are picking on you. That you're different. And while that doesn't feel like a real reason, it's a reason real enough for them. As a kid, you can watch all the movies and television specials you want . . . it can still be something you miss, when it's not explained to you.

After all, how do you teach someone to navigate the complexities of unjustified hatred when it's not a part of their personal, lived experience?

Instead of "boys will be boys" it might as well have been "racists will be racists."

As a transracial adoptee with very little identity, this was my problem. The lack of adult allies in my life was staggering. When I had questions about this for my family, they were usually answered with an awkward attempt at brushing it off, saying stuff like "it doesn't matter, you're all American" like we were in a really bad country song. But lyrics to an imaginary country song weren't going to solve why kids were picking on me for being different.

Sometimes in your search for allies, in your search for answers, you can discover them in places that surprise you.

For me, when the adults in my life were failing, not for lack of trying but because they just didn't know how, those allies were the friends I surrounded myself with. I didn't ask for help. Honestly, I don't think I knew that I needed it. They were the ones who swept in.

Sometimes I like to imagine them, sitting around a kitchen table after school or the lunch table while I was off practicing my saxophone for band, and deciding that this was going to be a goal of theirs. Like a bunch of Avengers. Help Eric figure it out. Give him some culture.

Show him a little of who we know he is by showing him who we are, and the reality of the world we live in together.

Growing up in Elizabeth, New Jersey, I was in a lucky place to be an adoptee struggling with identity, despite the bullying that happened. It's a vastly diverse city. My dearest friends came from all corners of the world. This was before the days of DNA kits you could send away for in the mail, there was no genetics testing app to download to make the mystery clear up. And New Jersey's adoption records laws were so wildly strict back then (they have since opened up and become way relaxed), that I never saw my own birth certificate until I was in my mid thirties.

Luckily for me, many of these friends from my childhood are still a massive part of my life, and it doesn't take much to get a clear picture of them in my head and my heart. Miguel, Darlene, Dario, Alberto, Liliana, Saray, Amy, Gabby, Danny . . . there's a wholesome list of people I grew up with, from those tumultuous days in junior high through college, who helped pull identity out of me, one piece at a time.

The time spent lingering outside the local corner store, venting about these big life issues, would grow over the next few years. From me opening up more about being bullied and adopted as a kid, to navigating identity as a teenager.

Come high school, my best friends were pushing me to play in an after-school Latin jazz band they had started. Me, the only member of the group who couldn't speak Spanish. They pressed music on me in long car rides home, stayed late with me after school so I could learn the rhythms. Miguel sat next to me, explaining the time signature differences in merengue vs. salsa, while I fought with my saxophone to stay on beat. I fondly remember Dario taking me aside into one of our school's few practice rooms, convinced he could teach me to sing in Spanish.

I did poorly, but that's not the point, is it?

"You should learn this," Dario would press, on late-night drives to grab fast food in an aging Thunderbird. We would sit there in KFC parking lots, eating chicken wraps with the radio on, while he talked to me about his family and culture and delicately found ways to get me to talk about mine . . . and guess about the mysteries I didn't have answers for.

We all had a table, as high school kids sometimes do, that we claimed as our own in the cafeteria. I remember everyone who sat around it, a few of whom are married to one another now nearly two decades later. Everyone speaking Spanish and taking the time to teach me phrases.

By then, the people who picked on me in junior high had mostly lost interest, for whatever reason. I like to think it's because of the people I surrounded myself with. My mind flashes to Vinny, and how the bullies tried to come knocking again in my high school life, and the way he just stood up. They walked away. That was all he had to do. Stand up.

Sometimes that's all you have to do.

IT WAS THROUGH TEACHING ME ABOUT THEIR OWN IDENTITIES THAT MY FRIENDS WERE ABLE TO HELP ME DISCOVER A SENSE OF MY OWN.

It was through teaching me about their own identities that my friends were able to help me discover a sense of my own. Lunch table talk, long drives, and attempts at starting bands aside, there were so many more examples of this kindness and allyship. I went to a wild amount of family parties and dinners. I danced in several quinceañeras as a member of the court. There were so many late-night dancing lessons in chilly basements, long drives our junior and senior years, talking about family and what that word meant. How in the many ways my family chose me, as an adoptee, I could also choose a family for myself.

We sipped coffee on college campuses long before we could even dream of being students there, discussing how it didn't matter to someone on the outside. Who didn't know my history, our history, was going to judge regardless of what I told them, or what I knew about myself.

In 2019, New Jersey decided to open up adoption records for adoptees. It was a complicated process that had the potential to be disappointing for many, because when you requested your information biological family was informed, and they could opt to have their information blotted out. In my case, the information was left there.

There were a few reasons for wanting answers on my end. The questions I'd spent my whole life asking, sure. The friends who gently suggested things, taught me about racism, they'd inspired me to look into all of this. And my wife and I were expecting our first child.

I didn't want him growing up with questions.

That didn't feel like an option for me as a soon-to-be parent who wrestled with that very same thing as a child. This circle wasn't something I was interested in repeating.

When the time came for me to finally open my birth certificate for the first time as an adult, and I saw where I was from, I called up all those friends.

"Hey so, it turns out I'm half Honduran."

I could hear their smiles through the phone lines.

Every single one of them said "I knew it."

And because of them, I'd spent years knowing it, too. I'd grown up understanding what racism was, and how to combat it. By diving into it, and absolutely embracing the thing that people were trying to use against me. Who I was. My identity, the culture that I wasn't raised with, but belonged to me.

Allyship comes in a lot of forms. It can be supporting a friend wrestling with microaggressions, standing up for a stranger on the bus, sharing your stance on social media. It can come in quiet invisible waves, through donations and the decisions you make for yourself, who you're supporting with what you buy and consume. It can come from people teaching you what that fight is that others are telling you to rethink.

Or it can come in the form of someone taking your hand and teaching you to salsa in a cold basement.

Sometimes the people who you expect to be the allies in your life will unfortunately fail you. Hopefully it's not through anything malicious, I don't wish that on anyone. It might just be because they're not sure what to do. And as the marginalized person, finding yourself in a position where you potentially have to teach people to be allies can be . . . undesirable. Particularly if they're the adults in your life you want fighting for you. And it's in those moments that I hope you'll search for answers in unexpected places . . . with the family you choose for yourself.

They're the ones who might just be able to tell you what that fight is you're "supposed" to walk away from.

And exactly why you shouldn't.

Because when it comes to choosing your battles, if the person you're fighting for is yourself? There are a few choices. The ones people want you to make, and the one you know is right.

Choose allies who choose you. And in the end, choose yourself.

4

ROUND AND ROUND WE GO

KAYLA WHALEY

I.

My first interview on the annual Jerry Lewis MDA Telethon lasted all of five minutes, maybe less. I was in third grade, seven years old. The host asked about my favorite classes, my family, my hobbies. I don't remember most of my answers, but I know I gave strategic ones. The audience needed to like me. They needed to think I was worth making a call for, so I turned my charm on high. I smiled just so and laughed at all the right times. I was witty, but never less than sincere. I was adorable, while hopefully never veering into precociousness. I used the interviewer's reactions to my answers as a stand-in for the audience's. If she was warming to me (and she was), everyone else would be, too.

The last question she asked was the same for every interviewee: "What would you say to people watching? What would their donation mean to you?"

I sobered. This was the moment. I'd either convince the viewers once and for all or drive them away. It wasn't a time for smiles. The lights were hot and my voice was loud in the silent ballroom as I stared into the camera lens, letting all those eyes on the other side stare into mine. I told them their donation would mean the world to me. With one simple phone call, they would let me attend summer camp, visit my doctor, get my flu shot, replace my wheelchair the next time I needed one. They would make my life better. I asked them to please, please, call and donate whatever they could spare. I asked them to help me, to help us, to help Jerry's Kids.

My speech wasn't particularly inspired, but it didn't need to be; it needed only be inspiring. As soon as the host threw back to the others, the phones rang. The whole bank of them all at once. Hundreds of bring-brings reaching across the ballroom. All of them for me. The host, beaming, leaned in and whispered, "This is the loudest it's been all day. You were wonderful. I doubt anyone could say no to you after that."

I left to a chorus of "how much can I put you down for?" and "thank you for helping Jerry's Kids."

I'd never been prouder in my life.

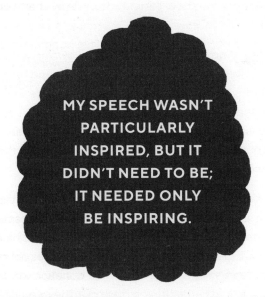

MY SPEECH WASN'T PARTICULARLY INSPIRED, BUT IT DIDN'T NEED TO BE; IT NEEDED ONLY BE INSPIRING.

II.

For nearly fifty years, the Telethon was the Muscular Dystrophy Association's annual fundraiser/spectacle. Every Labor Day weekend, comedian Jerry Lewis would host the event surrounded by celebrities, musicians, politicians, businessmen, and more. All to benefit us "Jerry's Kids." We were a constant fixture—as a group, if not as individuals. We were small, cute, mostly white, and all visibly disabled: the perfect poster children. MDA wasn't the first to use poster children or even the first to stage elaborate telethons, but they did have arguably the most success out of all the organizations that employed similar tactics.

Throughout its run, the Telethon raised almost two billion dollars. In its glory days, the show was an American staple with families across the country routinely tuning in over the holiday weekend. Many factors contributed to the Telethon's unprecedented success, from the never-ending celebrity guests to Lewis's (often criticized) shtick to the sheer magnitude of stations that carried the program.

But it would be a mistake to underestimate how integral Jerry's Kids were in the effort. Jerry Lewis was the name and face of the show, but we, his "kids," were the main attraction. We were the ones pulling the heartstrings and opening the wallets. We were the entire reason the funds needed raising in the first place. It's difficult to convince people to hand over their money without some proof of where it'll be going. We were the proof.

The Atlanta-area portion of the show was filmed on the ground floor of the Atlanta Airport Hilton in a large ballroom that had been converted to a filming set and phone bank for the duration of the weekend. Outside that room was a high-ceilinged atrium attached to a long, wide hallway leading in one direction back to the hotel proper and in the other to the greenroom, a generous name for a conference room filled with tables and a few rows of finger sandwiches, chips, and fruit. The tables were packed in tight, leaving little room for those of us who used wheelchairs to maneuver, so we mostly hung out in the atrium.

The majority of us were there to be interviewed, some of the older ones to help answer phones, but the Telethon was more to us than five minutes holding a microphone, more than a fundraiser. It was also a reunion.

Outside of summer camp, this was the only time of year that we all got together. The weeks before would see a flurry of Facebook messages and texts between campers and our counselors all saying something to the effect of "see you at Telethon, right?!"

My friends and I looked forward to the Telethon like an end-of-summer bash, which in many ways it was. The atmosphere outside the ballroom was always festive and energized. Every time another familiar face showed up, they were greeted with a wave of cheers and hugs. Our chatter and laughter filled the large atrium quickly and lasted all day, the sound echoing buoyantly around the chamber and its twenty-foot ceiling.

Once every hour, though, the ballroom doors closed, revealing the "LIVE TAPING" signs on the backs of them. We quieted immediately. The walls were so porous they might as well have been cheesecloth, so we knew not to risk even whispers when the national show threw to its local affiliates—to us. Not that that stopped us, of course. The MDA staffers standing outside the doors inevitably had to shush us a few times during the weekend. But what did they expect? We were kids hanging out with friends we only rarely got to see. A little rowdiness was only natural.

Besides, we were perfect angels when our faces were in front of the cameras.

III.

Plenty of former poster children have spoken out against the Telethon over the years. Activists have criticized, among other issues: the focus on children when the majority of MDA's clients are adults; the framing of disability as an inherent tragedy and disabled people as inherently tragic; Jerry Lewis's repeated dehumanizing statements about disabled people; and the dangerous fixation on an improbable "cure" rather than services that could improve quality of life.

And from a disability rights perspective, the use of poster children can reinforce ableist ideas of disability and the value (or lack thereof) of disabled lives. Consider MDA's #1 goal of finding a cure. What are they really saying? If the organization's mission is to better the lives of people with MD, and their primary focus is on eradicating MD, then they must believe that abled lives are automatically "better" and more worth living than disabled lives. The entire pitch relies on an assumed abled audience that fears disability or pities disabled people. Poster children require an abled gaze to be an effective tool.

AND MAKE NO MISTAKE: WE WERE TOOLS. I KNEW IT EVEN AS A CHILD, THOUGH I DIDN'T UNDERSTAND ALL THAT IT MEANT. AT THE TIME, I WANTED NOTHING MORE THAN TO BE USEFUL.

And make no mistake: we were tools. I knew it even as a child, though I didn't understand all that it meant. At the time, I wanted nothing more than to be useful. The adults organizing the event all doused me with praise, telling me how I was making a difference, helping the cause, leading the charge.

Being a poster child felt empowering. My actions and my voice were integral to this organization that made life better for kids like me, including me. That sense of agency was intoxicating, because as a physically disabled girl, I had something to prove—even before I had the language to understand it, let alone express it.

But tools don't wield themselves. Without someone to grasp them, guide them, use them, they are—we were—only objects. The power I felt was real, but it wasn't really mine. Or is that too easy? Too simplistic a view of the complicated exchanges (thefts? assignments? relinquishments?) of power at play?

> **BUT TOOLS DON'T WIELD THEMSELVES. WITHOUT SOMEONE TO GRASP THEM, GUIDE THEM, USE THEM, THEY ARE—WE WERE—ONLY OBJECTS. THE POWER I FELT WAS REAL, BUT IT WASN'T REALLY MINE.**

We can't forget about the other side of this exchange either. All those people watching at home, the local businesses that raised money for weeks or months leading up to the event, every single person who donated over fifty years. Those people and their actions didn't just benefit the organization or "Jerry's Kids." The people acting benefited, too. They got to feel proud, generous, helpful, like an agent of change, or a steward for good.

They got to feel like allies.

But I can't think about that feel-good glow without also thinking of the people watching me, picking up their phones at my request, donating their money on my behalf, and feeling satisfied with themselves, even as I also felt satisfied with my own self.

The usual arguments against the use of poster children chafe at me. Not because I disagree with them, but because there's something missing from those arguments that renders them unexpectedly hollow. I'd call that something the children's agency, but did we actually have agency in any meaningful way? If I pull back and approach the question from a distance, the answer must surely be no.

When abled adults—and especially abled authority figures, like the parents who ultimately had to grant or deny permission for our involvement—ask disabled children to participate in a fundraising effort, those children hold no power in that situation. Without relational power, can one claim control over their own choices? Is assent to participate the same thing as consent? If it is and we did indeed consent, was it truly informed? And if it wasn't informed, was it truly consent?

I GO IN CIRCLES.

But here again, I bristle. That we were children and that we were disabled might mean we lacked relational power, but it doesn't mean we were powerless.

I go in circles: I reject the implication that my choice was an illusion, that I was manipulated (however unintentionally) into participating, even while I accept that my decision was formed largely by ableist ideas about usefulness and worth that would have made me exceptionally easy to manipulate.

IV.

I enjoyed being a
poster child. It might
have only been local
public broadcasting, but it
felt meaningful. It felt good.
Those are positive memories for me.
They are firmly wrapped in fondness.

I STILL CAN'T DECIDE IF I CONSENTED OR NOT.

Does that make me a hypocrite? If harm is
only visible in retrospect, does that make it any
less valid?

I didn't know there was a difference between being useful
and being used; being seen and being consumed; being
different and being Other.

Nuance wasn't something I was equipped to see. I was seven
years old. They asked me to be on TV. They told me I could help.
They showed me I was valued. Of course, my value came only
from my disability. My wheelchair and the physical weakness
of my body, those were valuable. Those were my defining
characteristics, and the only ones worth anything—because
they were worth something to abled people.

But I used them, too, didn't I? I played off their expectations
and biases—without even the benefit of being able to name
those things yet—and convinced them to give up their money.
I acted in a way that strategically and specifically relied on and
(however unconsciously) reinforced ableist ideas of disability
and disabled people.

I still can't decide if I consented or not.

I go in circles.

Perhaps that's all there is: circles of exploitation and complicity and good intentions and benefits and harm. Circles of abled adults using disabled children who grow into disabled adults who have to reckon with having been used as disabled children.

I like to think there's more, though. I like to think it's possible to help others, and ourselves, without dehumanizing them, or us.

I need to believe that while I was undoubtedly used, my shining memories of the Telethon—being interviewed, visiting friends, being seen by the anonymous and seemingly infinite others watching from behind their screens—can withstand the rust that age and understanding have both mercilessly and mercifully brought to them.

V.

A few years ago, my dad went to get Munchkins from Dunkin' Donuts like he did every Saturday morning. That day he had happened to take our accessible van instead of his truck, not an unusual occurrence. A little more than halfway to the store, a car in the opposite lane didn't curve with the road and hit Dad head-on. His injuries were minor (though he wound up dealing with chronic pain for years), but the van was totaled.

Accessible vans are expensive. The cost of the modifications are tens of thousands of dollars on top of the regular cost of the vehicle. Replacing it was going to be rough, but the short-term was an even more pressing problem. That van was my only mode of transportation. Without it, I had no way to leave the house. None. I was well and truly trapped. Our only option was to rent a van while we sorted out replacing ours, but we didn't have thousands of dollars on hand for an extended rental. So I did what any good millennial would do: I asked the Internet for help.

I agonized over how to write the GoFundMe description. Should I keep it journalistic, or aim for an emotional response?

> **SO I DID WHAT ANY GOOD MILLENNIAL WOULD DO: I ASKED THE INTERNET FOR HELP.**

How much should I focus on being "housebound" without a car?

Will that turn people off because it sounds melodramatic? Will it make them pity me? Do I maybe want them to pity me if it means more donations? Should I pull on those years of Telethon experience and pluck at the proverbial heartstrings once again, my one-time specialty?

In the end, I went with simple but honest: "... my only form of transportation.

... the van was totaled.... several weeks at least before we can move forward with securing a new vehicle.

... The best option we've found for rentals costs $90/day plus tax when renting for a month.

... would sincerely appreciate any and all help."

People started giving immediately. Five dollars, ten dollars, fifty dollars, even $1,000 in one case (my mom almost fainted at that one). From friends, followers, complete strangers. Most donations were sent with some short message of support. And they just kept coming. The relief was overwhelming. Not just because we might actually be able to afford a rental, but because so many people had my back without hesitation.

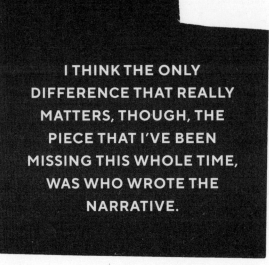

I THINK THE ONLY DIFFERENCE THAT REALLY MATTERS, THOUGH, THE PIECE THAT I'VE BEEN MISSING THIS WHOLE TIME, WAS WHO WROTE THE NARRATIVE.

I needed help, I asked for help, and people helped.

It really was that simple.

There are obviously a lot of differences between me, an individual, asking for donations to solve a very specific, short-term problem, and a national organization fundraising for a year's worth of massive programming. But the basic tactics for each were the same: a disabled girl asking for money from a (largely) abled audience. The scale, scope, goals, and medium used were vastly different, but at the heart of both was the same plea: "Help me."

I think the only difference that really matters, though, the piece that I've been missing this whole time, was who wrote the narrative. Because when I ask for help for myself, for things that I need, in the way that I choose, framing my needs the way that feels appropriate to me—I'm not a tool anymore, I'm a person. And the people who help me aren't an audience for me to entice or wallets for me to open, they're people, too.

I still don't have all the answers. The questions about childhood agency, power dynamics, the abled gaze, they all still bother me.

I turn them over again and again and again. Even while writing this essay, I changed my mind a hundred times. I doubt myself. I doubt others. I go in circles.

But of this, I feel certain: it's only when we come together with our personhood intact on both sides that true allyship is possible. Maybe that's why raising the money for the rental didn't make me feel powerful so much as loved. And maybe now that I know better what allyship feels like, I'll be able to know better what it should look like, too.

THIS IS WHAT IT FEELS LIKE

A.J. SASS

FALL

. . . feels like summer everywhere else, because weather in the Bay Area, California, is just as quirky as the residents who call it home.

What it doesn't feel like? Pride season.

But because of the overwhelming popularity of San Francisco's Pride event in June—where a million visitors flood the streets over a single, celebratory weekend—September is when neighboring Oakland holds its festivities.

That's where I find myself one sun-kissed fall afternoon. My friends and I have chosen to picnic at a park close to the official Oakland Pride parade route. Owen (he/him) sits by my side, his bleached blond hair shaved short.

There are others in our group, virtually every shade of queer identity present and accounted for. Most are folks I met at a group therapy session for trans and questioning young adults a few months earlier.

We talk about our jobs (overworked, underpaid), the weather (finally warm after a frigid, foggy summer), the upcoming presidential election (Obama versus Romney). All the while,

I wait for a lull in the conversation, for my chance to share a vital piece in what feels like the increasingly complex puzzle of my life.

I've psyched myself out before, back in June during the San Francisco Trans March. That's when Owen revealed his new name. I didn't want to dilute his news with my own announcement.

But in the months since the Trans March, the thought of sharing my own new name has grown into something bigger, scarier.

I take a breath as Dom (she/her) peels back the lid of a salsa container and her boyfriend, Oak (he/him), tosses Owen a bag of tortilla chips.

One long exhalation, then a rush of words. "I think I've figured out my name."

Their focus shifts. All eyes on me. My chest flutters, like a butterfly trapped in a mason jar.

Sharing a new name feels permanent, irreversible, but also necessary. Among friends, I am A (who-the-heck-knows-yet on pronouns), the first initial of my birth name. I haven't gotten that far with my coworkers, resigning myself to prickling discomfort every time they unknowingly misgender me.

I could shrug this off with a laugh and a quick shake of my head. Never mind. Just kidding.

Except, I don't want to take a step back. It's exhausting to juggle multiple identities.

"I'm going with Andrew." I swallow hard. "I think?"

Not the confident declaration I envisioned, but at least it's out.

"Cool." Owen leans forward, dipping a chip into our communal salsa. "You know you can always change it later, too, if you end up not liking it."

THE BUTTERFLY IN MY CHEST FLIES UP, THEN OUT THROUGH MY RIBS. THE JAR WAS A TEMPORARY PRISON. IT NEVER HAD A LID TO BEGIN WITH.

A contingent of parade participants snakes toward us on the street below our hill. Music starts up. Heavy bass thrums in my throat.

"Yeah?"

"Totally. I must've tried half a dozen names before I landed on Owen."

It seems so obvious now that he's said it, but still. You don't know what you don't know.

"I was Pine for, like, two weeks a few years ago," Oak offers. "But it always made me think of the cleaning solution."

Owen laughs, then nudges me. "Andrew for now, though?"

The butterfly in my chest flies up, then out through my ribs. The jar was a temporary prison. It never had a lid to begin with.

I nod as hundreds of rainbow flags flutter below us. "Andrew for now."

Fall feels like a fresh start, so full of potential.

WINTER

... feels like time to write a novel.

For years, that's exactly what I do. Every November, I commit to writing a minimum of 1,667 words per day to hit the fabled 50K that makes you a winner of National Novel Writing Month (NaNoWriMo).

If you live in the Bay Area (or are willing to travel here), you can even attend the noir-themed Night of Writing Dangerously, NaNoWriMo's annual fundraiser.

The Julia Morgan Ballroom is a lavish venue in San Francisco's Financial District: tall ceilings, thick velvet curtains, golden crown molding. I'd attended last year, but that was different. It was pre-transition, when I had another job, accompanied by a former partner.

This is the first time I'm here on my own, decked out in suspenders, a small-brim fedora, and Oxford button-up. Authentically Andrew—or at least a little closer.

I choose a seat at one of a dozen round tables. A stack of name tags forms the centerpiece. I fill one out, then press it onto my chest, just over my heart. Right now, most people are mingling with old friends or browsing a buffet table filled with every type of candy imaginable. Others are at the bar, ordering drinks with clever writing pun names.

I set up my laptop, preparing for a night of writing sprints on my fragmentary draft of a YA sci-fi story.

"Are these seats free?"

Another Wrimo writer looks down at me, wearing a similar outfit to mine (minus suspenders). A tie holds back sleek, black hair in a loose ponytail.

I nod. Watch them lean toward the center of the table, then fill out a name tag: Grace.

Grace waves at someone by the bar. Two someones, actually. Each drops a laptop bag at their feet, then fills out a name tag.

Tall, dark-haired Mark takes a seat beside Grace, across the table from me. I receive a small nod, then both settle in.

A glimpse of the other Wrimo makes my stomach twist. I don't have to look at her name tag to remember short, curly-haired Tammy. We shared a table last year, back before I was Andrew, or even A.

She knows me by my birth name.

Maybe it's the dim lighting, or my shorter hair, but Tammy doesn't say anything that implies she recognizes me. We say a round of hellos, then everyone unpacks their laptops and notebooks. I allow myself to relax a little.

It doesn't last long.

Because Mark keeps glancing at me from under the rim of his fedora. By now, the scrutiny feels familiar. I get looks like this often enough, even in progressive, come-as-you-are San Francisco.

I hunch over my laptop and adjust my hat so it covers more of my face, wishing people didn't have the inherent need to categorize every little thing.

Right | Wrong

Taken | Single

Boy | Girl

In some ways, I get it. I know categories help avoid confusion. I also know that a traditionally boy's name stuck to my chest

doesn't address all the other aspects of my appearance that imply the opposite.

I wait for the question I know is coming. My suspenders weigh down on my tense shoulders.

"Hey," Mark says. "Pass me that marker."

By the time I look up, Grace has already handed it over. Mark strips off his name tag in one smooth motion, scribbles something, then puts it back on.

I blink at his tag:

Mark

He, him, his

Mark catches me looking. "I'm usually way more on top of these things."

My tension drains away as Grace adds *she/her* to her name tag, then passes the marker to Tammy. The *she* + *her* isn't a surprise to me here, but it's still nice to know for sure.

The marker reaches me. I write a careful *he*, trying it on for size. Since quitting my job earlier this month, I haven't been thinking about pronouns as much, but I know I'll eventually have to figure them out.

This time when Mark looks at me, he smiles instead of furrowing his brows.

A Night of Writing Dangerously organizer steps up to a podium, then announces the first official writing sprint of the night. Our focus shifts to our notebooks and laptops, heads bowed, fingers a rapid blur. Every second matters. Each word counts.

Throughout the evening, we chat about our novels, what part of the city we live in, what we do with our lives when we're not trying to write a manuscript in such a short span of time. Dinner comes and goes. We get up and stretch, have author portraits taken by a professional photographer, and listen to inspirational speeches from fellow Wrimos.

As midnight approaches, we grab milk and cookies before the final sprint. I trade numbers with all three of them, setting up a time to meet Mark later in the week to write together.

When the event ends, I say goodbye to Mark and Grace who head off in one direction. Tammy and I walk the other way together.

"Want to share a taxi?" I ask her.

She shakes her head. "I'm walking distance. But I'll wait with you."

It's not long before my taxi rolls up. I wave to Tammy, then pull open the door.

"Hey, Andrew," she says.

I turn back to her.

"Your new name suits you well."

Winter feels like a friendly nod. Like validation.

SPRING

. . . feels like a last-ditch attempt to fulfill winter resolutions.

That's why I accept when Mark invites me to work out at his gym one day in early April—even though the thought forms a thick knot in my stomach.

It's not that I haven't wanted to work out since I joined a gym in January. It's that bodies tell stories; mine wasn't telling the right one to a patron in the men's locker room at my last gym.

Are you trying to make a political statement or something?

His voice still echoes in my mind, although I wasn't even stripping down like everyone else. I'd worn shorts under my street clothes, not that it mattered.

His tone was clear: You don't belong.

Mark's gym is on the same street as mine. Located in San Francisco's famously gay Castro neighborhood, this stretch of Market Street is dotted with them. I'm not convinced trading one gym for another will be an improvement, but Mark and I have gotten close over the past few months, when I was between full-time jobs. While he sipped black coffee and worked on his novel at various cafes, I hunkered down with a sugary latte, writing freelance blog posts. Grace sometimes joined us.

Now I've got a new job, where I finally get to be myself. Correct name, male pronouns, thanks to a supportive boss. I can't make our weekday writing meetups anymore, so working out is one of the only times Mark and I can spend together.

Except that question-that-wasn't-really-a-question still gnaws at me.

As we take the stairs up to Mark's gym, my mind floods with belated comebacks.

My favorite:

I leave the politics for my ballot, thanks. Right now, I'm just trying to change.

Admittedly not great, but it's much better than what actually happened. I'd frozen, managing a barely audible "no," before escaping to the nearest bathroom stall.

Mark doesn't know this. I've kept it to myself like a shameful secret.

Now, I can't help giving him an out.

"Should I use the women's locker room here?"

Mark pauses in front of the entrance. "Do you want to use the women's locker room?"

I shake my head as he holds the door open for me.

> **BODIES TELL STORIES, WHETHER WE WANT THEM TO OR NOT. I CAN'T HELP WONDERING WHAT STORY MINE WILL TELL IF I START TAKING TESTOSTERONE.**

"So you'll use the men's," he says, like that settles it.

He signs me in as his guest, then we make our way into the locker room.

Inside, we pass a line of showers, separated by tile walls. This room is much smaller than the one at my gym. It's just an open space with a row of lockers. Nowhere to go if someone doesn't want me in here.

We're alone, for now. Not taking a second for granted, I change clothes as fast as I can. My workout shorts are already beneath my jeans, a sports bra and baggy T-shirt under my hoodie.

Out in the gym, Mark and I warm up on treadmills. Then he walks me through proper free-weight lifting technique.

I study Mark's every movement, memorizing not just the technique but also his body's contours. Wide at his shoulders, Mark's waist tapers like an upside-down triangle. I'm the opposite, with a slender upper body that goes wide at my hips.

Bodies tell stories, whether we want them to or not. I can't help wondering what story mine will tell if I start taking testosterone. Owen started months ago and already seems happy with his results. I'm still on the fence.

This time we're not alone when we return to the locker room.

"Want to grab some dinner?" Mark asks.

"Sure."

He peels off his sweaty shirt, either unaware of the two guys changing nearby or else unconcerned.

And why would he be? His body tells a straightforward story. Mine's full of plot twists.

He grabs a pair of towels and passes me one. "All good?"

Throat dry, I take the towel with a quick nod.

He heads off toward the showers. I turn away from the other two guys but can't make myself strip down like Mark did. Instead, I tuck my clean clothes under one arm and practically sprint to the nearest empty shower stall.

Only once I've confirmed the curtain is completely closed do I slip out of my clothes. I hang everything up on the metal curtain rod, then clean up.

By the time I'm done, Mark's already back in the locker area, voice drifting to me as he chats with another gym patron. I slide into my underwear and jeans, then look down at myself. Bare-chested, I don't look like any guy I've ever seen.

But maybe I'm reading this book all wrong. Maybe my chest isn't telling the story of a girl. What if it's just saying "Andrew?"

I drape the towel over my shoulders, then step out of the shower before I can second-guess myself. The towel's terrycloth ends mostly cover my chest.

This is a test, I decide. An experiment. I make my way back to the lockers.

Immediate regret. Now there are three guys.

"Hey, Andrew," Mark says as I drop my sweaty clothes on a bench. "This is Chris."

We exchange quick greetings, then Chris claims a locker across the room. It's only when I've shoved all my used clothes into my duffel bag that I realize I've made a fatal error in my calculations: I'm going to have to drop the towel to put on my shirt—unless I want to put it on over a wet towel, which, gross.

Mark takes a seat, then pulls out his phone. "I'm going to check if Grace wants to grab food with us."

A quick glance around shows no one's looking at me. I take my chance, letting the towel slide off my shoulders. In the same motion, I reach for my shirt, fumbling with the collar as I try to figure out which side is the front. My pulse pounds in my ears.

"How do you feel about sushi?"

I startle and the shirt drops to the bench. Cheeks burning, I can't bring myself to look over at Mark, or even cover myself up. This feels just like my last gym trip, except instead of politics, my downfall today is raw fish.

My shirt rises into view. I glance over at it, then down the length of Mark's arm. Our eyes meet. He's looking at me like normal. We could be in line at a store, waiting for the light to turn at a crosswalk. Anywhere.

"Sushi's fine." I try to put my shirt on at a normal speed but I'm probably still rushing. Chris gives me a quick smile as he heads out of the locker room. The other two aren't looking my way at all. I'm just one of the guys to them, getting changed after a workout.

All because Mark's treating me like one.

My pulse gradually slows.

Mark stands, swinging his duffel over one shoulder. "Grace said she can meet us in ten."

SPRING FEELS LIKE PERMISSION TO BE MYSELF, NO MATTER WHAT STORY OTHERS THINK MY BODY TELLS.

This time, I hold the door open for him when we exit the gym.

He looks over at me as we take the stairs down to Market Street. "So, what did you think?"

I take a breath of the air, still crisp with a final hint of winter. "I think I'm going to be switching gyms."

Spring feels like permission to be myself, no matter what story others think my body tells.

SUMMER

. . . feels like one long party, starting with Pride Month in June.

June is also when I take my first dose of testosterone, under the supervision of my doctor. A month later, my friends throw me a "T-party" in San Francisco's Dolores Park to celebrate the milestone. Mark is out of town, but Grace comes, as do Owen, Oak, and a handful of other people I've met at various events.

It's unusually warm for a July in the city and the afternoon feels festive. We're not the only ones picnicking on this gorgeous, sun-drenched day, but we've carved out a little space for ourselves, under the shade of a tree.

> THE TRANS GUY LABEL FEELS LIKE IT FITS ME ABOUT AS WELL AS A T-SHIRT THAT'S THREE SIZES TOO SMALL.

"So, explain why this guy you're dating thought he needed to call 911 after your T shot?" Owen pops one of Grace's homemade kale chips into his mouth. "I feel like I only got half of the story from your texts."

"It wasn't his fault." I try to hide my smile.

"I just didn't know some syringes have needles that auto-retract. The ones my doctor used definitely didn't."

Owen and Oak both nod. Apparently I'm the only one who didn't get the memo.

"So, it was my first time injecting at home and everything was going fine. But then the needle just disappeared after I pushed the plunger completely down." I shake my head, mildly embarrassed. "He wasn't the only one freaking out. I seriously thought I'd broken the needle off in my leg."

Laughter erupts from my friends.

"What a first date," Oak crows.

"Technically," I deadpan, "it was our third."

Owen nudges me. "Trans guy problems, right?"

A twinge of discomfort. Even though we're going through many of the same steps to medically transition, the trans guy label feels like it fits me about as well as a T-shirt that's three sizes too small.

"Something like that."

"So." Owen refills his paper cup with iced tea. "Have you noticed any changes yet?"

I side-eye him. "After a month?"

"Hey, you could be an early bloomer!"

"I'm not." Another twinge. "And honestly? I don't even know if I feel like a man yet."

"Give it time. It'll happen," Oak says. He's been on T the longest of all of us. "Especially when people stop misgendering you."

I reach for Grace's kale chips.

"I didn't believe it either," Owen tells me, "but it's definitely a thing. Just a few more months and you'll see."

He takes off his shirt and lays back, using it as a headrest. Faint scars smile up at me from under both of his pecs, the result of his top surgery a few months back. They've healed nicely, now barely noticeable. I wonder how my chest will look after my own surgery, scheduled for this fall.

I nod but don't respond. Time might change a lot of things, but I've been waiting all year for my feelings to shift on a similar trajectory with my body. They haven't. "Woman" isn't the right word for me, but "man" doesn't fit perfectly either.

And lately, I've been getting so frustrated with how binary the world feels.

Bathrooms and locker rooms.

Clothes.

Even computers speak in ones and zeros.

Oak waves a Frisbee and Owen gets up to join him for a game. Grace scoots closer to me. I sit with her in comfortable silence as thoughts swirl in my mind.

"Everything okay?"

"Sure." I shrug. "Why wouldn't it be?"

She takes a sip from her paper cup. "Just checking. You went quiet."

I sigh. Chew on a kale chip.

"I seriously don't think I'll ever feel like a man," I finally tell her, "even if I'm on T for years."

"Okay." She sits with this for a beat. "Well, maybe you aren't one. Just because Owen and Oak had similar experiences doesn't mean yours isn't valid because it's been different."

I don't know what she means, but her words immediately calm me.

"Now." Grace lays her head on my shoulder. "Tell me about this guy you've been seeing . . ."

Summer suddenly feels full of possibilities.

A YEAR

. . . feels like progress, but not as much as I thought it would.

It's easy to look back now, years later, armed with the knowledge that transition looks different for every trans person. There is no one right way to discover who you are.

When I first came out as a transgender, I hadn't heard the term "non-binary" yet. Plus, all the trans narratives I could find online talked about knowing who you are from a young age. Even my own friends said they knew when they were kids.

That wasn't my experience.

A year after Oakland Pride, the Night of Writing Dangerously, my renewed commitment to workouts, and the Dolores Park T-party, I will hear the term non-binary for the first time. I'll let its definition build in my mind—not relating to, composed of, or involving just two things—until I can see the shape of it. Until I recognize it for what it's always been.

An image of myself, reflecting back at me.

Two years later, I will leave my beloved San Francisco for a small town where no one knows my background. I'll settle into the labels others give me because being seen as a gay man seems

> FOR THE FIRST TIME, A LABEL
> WILL FEEL LIKE IT FITS
> PROPERLY; RATHER THAN
> SETTLING FOR TERMS OTHERS
> GIVE ME, THIS WORD WILL
> BECOME A POINT OF PRIDE THAT
> I'LL CLAIM AS MINE . . .

less complicated for people to grasp than being trans. My friends and I will try to keep in touch, although some of us will grow apart.

Five years from now, I'll write a book about a non-binary ice skater. It'll feel liberating to explore the gendered components of a sport I've trained in since I was a kid. Grace will read it, provide feedback. I'll query literary agents and sign with one I'm excited to work with.

As my agent prepares my manuscript for submission to publishers, she'll ask if I'm comfortable with her pitching me as a non-binary author. She'll tell me she supports me no matter my decision.

Six years, and that book will sell. I'll share the news on social media and come out to my friends and family for a second time.

I will make the decision to discontinue testosterone and update my pronouns. Expand them, actually, making room alongside he, his, him for they, their, them. I'll feel a small thrill whenever people use them interchangeably to refer to me.

The guy I met six summers ago, now my boyfriend, will embrace these changes. Same for my friends. They'll offer to throw me another party, although distance precludes it becoming reality.

Eight years, and I'll become a debut author, penning essays about my journey to discovering I'm non-binary. For the first time, a label will feel like it fits properly; rather than settling for terms others give me, this word will become a point of pride that I'll claim as mine, wholeheartedly. During my virtual book launch event, I'll get asked a question by an eleven-year-old non-binary kid about what it's like to live in the world as a non-binary adult. This is the moment I'll finally know that my struggles to define myself on my own terms have been worth it.

A year might not feel like a long time, but years add up.

Every single one has brought me closer to the person I am now.

6

A BUS, A POSTER, AND A MIRROR

BRENDAN KIELY

I have to tell you about the time I was a real @&$^*%#.

It's like this.

I grew up outside of Boston, Massachusetts, and in seventh grade, the entire class, all 300 or so of us, took a field trip to Washington, D.C. I don't know what the heck our teachers and parents were thinking. Of course nothing would go wrong, right? Of course none of us would get into any trouble—right? Of course we'd listen to everything the adults told us to do . . .

Of course NOT!

Honestly, I'm surprised there wasn't more trouble. It was middle school, there was mayhem, and I don't remember much of the trip—I don't even know what museums we went to or how many days we were there. But I do remember Z.

He was a big kid, pudgy. And his voice seemed too high and goofy. He wasn't trying to sound cool, or "more like a man," like so many of us guys were. He missed social cues. He didn't get the jokes we all made. He'd suddenly go quiet and seem lost in his own thoughts, and then, when he came back to life, he was too loud.

What he had to say was a response to a joke or a comment someone made three minutes earlier, so the timing was all off. He had thick, dark glasses that made his deep brown eyes look bigger than a deer's—and most often, that's what he looked like—the old deer-stunned-and-staring-into-headlights cliché. His hair never looked washed, and it lay slick and messy over his head like a pile of sticks gone mushy with decay.

That's a pretty mean description of him, actually. I bet his mother never would have described him that way. But I guess I remember him in a mean way because I was mean to him on the trip.

Other kids made jokes about his name. They played pranks on him at meals. They made fun of the way he talked. Someone tried to point him in the wrong direction at one of the museums so he might get lost. Many kids were mean to him. And I was, too.

I laughed when people did all these things. I laughed at the jokes and the preying on him, the attempt to get him lost. And then one time, I was more than just another mean kid in the crowd. I was the big, bad bully himself.

One night on the bus ride back to the hotel, I found myself sitting in a seat behind Z. A couple of my friends were beside me and we were teasing Z behind his back. We'd say something to get him all riled up, just to watch him get frustrated. My buddy flicked his ear. I laughed. Then, I poked my finger into his hair to see if it would stand up on its own. A gooey clump of his greasy hair just stood straight up in the air for a while and Z didn't even notice. My friends and I laughed, but the clump slowly drooped back down to his head. I was chomping a wad of bubblegum, and as I started to blow a bubble an idea hit me.

I pulled the gum out of my mouth with two fingers. It was bright and enormous like a birthday balloon and it smelled like fruit

> **AT THE TIME, I THOUGHT I WAS A COMEDIAN. IT WAS ALL A JOKE. CAN'T PEOPLE JUST TAKE A JOKE? (OOOOH. REMEMBER THAT LINE. BECAUSE WE'RE DEFINITELY GOING TO COME BACK TO IT LATER.)**

grown in a lab with electricity and battery acid instead of water and soil. And I pushed up a clump of Z's hair and pressed the wad of gum into it with my thumb.

Z's hair stood straight in the air, as if someone had grabbed a few of those sticks from the pile and stuck them into the ground like flagpoles.

I think I laughed so hard I snorted.

Like an animal.

Like something that doesn't really belong in the company of other people because he does more to harm other people than he does help other people.

At the time, I thought I was a comedian. It was all a joke. Can't people just take a joke? (Ooooh. Remember that line. Because we're definitely going to come back to it later.)

Because, in fact, it wasn't a joke. What was so pathetic about the way we teased Z, was that we belittled him to make ourselves feel better about . . . well . . . ourselves.

And there was a kid sitting next to Z who understood this, who didn't think what I'd done to Z was funny at all. He didn't want to "take it" as a joke any more than Z did. Colin—one of the most popular guys in our grade. I'd known him in elementary school, too. He was a football AND a baseball star. He'd had girlfriends on and off since fifth grade. We'd wrestled once in his front yard and I'd quickly realized I would literally never be able to beat him.

But most importantly, he was a good person.

He turned around and looked at me and my friends and asked, "Who did this?"

He looked annoyed, but also sad. He shook his head and he asked us again. He didn't sound like the rest of us. In fact, he sounded like an adult, and when his eyes landed on me, and he asked his question for the third time—that's when I knew I wasn't cool. That's when I knew I wasn't funny. That's when I knew I was an @$&#%**.

I also realized that Colin might have decided to sit next to Z on purpose. I'd seen Colin with him at the museum where Z almost got lost. I'd seen Colin standing between Z and some of the other kids who'd been teasing Z earlier on the trip when we were in line to get our pictures taken on the National Mall. But I hadn't put two and two together until he nosed forward over the bus seat and squinted at me when he asked me, "Why would you do that to him?"

I mumbled my excuses, trying to say something about it being "no big deal," that it was "only a joke." But I felt gutted and shallow, a liar getting caught in his own lie.

"Nah. It's not funny," Colin continued. "How do you think he feels?"

I couldn't say exactly, but if it felt anything like how I felt when Colin called me out, I knew it felt terrible. And I wasn't even getting picked on—I was simply getting called out—once.

"And you're an @$&#*%^, Brendan."

He was right.

The next day, I learned that Colin had invited Z to his hotel room and he'd made all his roommates help him try to get the gum out of Z's hair. Eventually, they had to cut some of his hair with scissors, and then, because it was uneven, they'd figured out how to give him a full haircut.

It was short. It was out of his eyes. It looked good.

The bullying ended.

Not because of his hair, obviously. Because Colin intervened and made sure Z wasn't alone to defend himself.

How do you think he feels? There was something about that question that blew down deep inside and whistled through my bones. And I still hear it, again and again, all these years later, no matter where I am or what I'm doing, or who I'm with. I look around and see how people are treating each other, how the people in the room are treating people who aren't in the room, and the question Colin asked me that day echoes in my mind. How do you think they feel?

But that question isn't enough. It's only half the story. If I just sit there thinking about how other people are feeling but I remain silent when they're getting picked on, trash talked about, attacked, or bullied in any way—yeah, I might not be the @$&^*!# who is causing all the pain, but I still might be an @$& for not doing anything to try to stop it.

The part of my story about the bus is pretty simple. I was a bully and Colin stepped in to stop me. So what about when the story is more complicated? What about when the bullying isn't seen as bullying, or it's seen as "normal" behavior, so when no one stops it, someone (or many people) are getting hurt, but no one is even talking about it?

My story gets more complicated like that. And so it goes on like this . . .

After middle school, my parents yanked me away from all of my friends and sent me to an all-boys Catholic high school.

THEY WERE TALKING ABOUT THOSE GIRLS AS THOUGH THE PERSON DIDN'T EXIST—ONLY THE BODY DID.

That's right. There were no girls at my high school. It was about 1,000 boys jockeying for social positioning in a very, very different kind of environment than I was used to. I was used to walking the halls with girls; being partnered with girls for group projects; and hanging out with girls before school, in class, at lunch, and after school. But at my high school, none of that happened. Instead, the classrooms, the cafeteria, the parking lots, the athletic fields—everywhere—we, the students, the guys, just talked about girls.

We talked about girls in the minutes before the bell rang in class. We talked about girls in the hallways, in gym class, in the parking lots, in the locker room—everywhere. Constantly talking about people who aren't in the room can get a little weird. A conversation about folks, when they aren't there to speak up, too often turns into an opportunity for the talk to turn mean—especially when a group of guys are just sitting around talking about girls.

Because they weren't talking about the girls as people, about Shanice, or Julie, or Tiffany, or Carol, or Maria, or whomever. They were talking about those girls as though the person didn't exist—only the body did.

I had a hard time navigating these conversations. In fact, the conversations made me nervous. If this is how these guys feel about girls when the girls aren't in the room—how can it be any different how they feel about the girls when the girls are actually in the room?

On the one hand, I wanted to fit in and make new friends. I wanted to feel like I belonged at the school, because I was stuck there anyway, so I wanted to make the best of it. And so I listened. I didn't try to stop any of the conversation. I didn't stop any of the comments—not even the really rude ones, not even the ones that sounded most aggressive and demeaning.

But on the other hand, I felt myself standing there, listening to what these guys were talking about and feeling a windstorm of uncomfortable on the inside. Somewhere, deep down, I knew all this degrading talk about women and girls was wrong. In fact, it reminded me a lot of what it felt like when we were bullying Z back on that field trip in seventh grade.

The way these guys talked about girls was a way to puff themselves up and feel better about themselves. They clung to the bonkers idea that the way to demonstrate just how "manly" they were was to think less of women, objectify them, demean them, and talk about what they would do to them. They thought they were showing off how "tough," how "strong," how "hard" they were, because they felt like that was how you were supposed to "prove" that you were a man—but all they really were was cruel and dangerous!

Because hey. Real talk: any kind of sexual act, even something as simple as a kiss, is an act you do with someone—which means the other person has to want to do it, too—which means the other person has to tell you he or she wants to do it, too. Yup. You have to hear it out loud. "Yes." It's called consent.

What these guys were saying—how they were acting—all of it

grossed me out. And I had to ask myself if I was the same Brendan on the bus in D.C., or if I was a different Brendan—one who thought about other human beings as actual . . . Other. Human. Beings.

But that was the wrong question. I better not have been the same Brendan on the bus—he was a jerk! And I wasn't, exactly. I didn't engage in those bullying conversations about girls with guys at my school. I didn't demean and belittle girls. But I also didn't say anything to stop the other guys from speaking that way. What I mean is, I should have asked myself if I was more like the Colin on the bus now—willing to turn around and say something to the bullies.

But I didn't ask myself that question. Because the only answer to it was no. Even though I wasn't an outright bully, I sure was still a freaking whole lot more like the Brendan on the bus than the Colin on the bus. Oh no!

Oh yes.

You mean staying silent about bullying behavior you witness and hear is complicit with the bullying behavior?

That's exactly right.

Oh no.

Oh, very much yes.

Now, there were some girls I had grown up with, some girls I was still friends with back home, and some girls I was meeting through a network of new friends in high school who, if they'd been in the room when those degrading comments started flying around, would have called those guys on it. They would have confronted the guys head on, without backing down. But there were plenty of girls who wouldn't want to take fire from these boys, too. I definitely don't speak for them or any woman, but that was the point—there weren't any girls there. No girls in our locker room. No girls in our gym class. No girls in our parking lot after school.

I was. And a lot of other guys were, too. And we did nothing. We said nothing.

I wasn't an ally—I was a coward. In fact, many of us were cowards—too many of us.

But as I got older, maybe I did become a little more like Colin on the bus than the Brendan on the bus.

By my senior year, I certainly felt a little more comfortable making sure guys around me knew I didn't appreciate any kind of BS misogynistic remarks. Or, even if I didn't feel comfortable, at least I knew I had to say something if I heard someone starting to get offensive and demeaning. And I'd speak up. It wasn't much. Maybe a simple, "Hey, enough of that." And then I'd get heckled, but at least it distracted them from saying wild stuff about women.

But, come on. You know that wasn't enough.

And this, I think, is where my story gets more complicated.

Remember? I said it was more complicated.

(Psst: Here's the part about the poster, too.)

In the month leading up to our senior prom, a clothing store at the mall was allowed to hang advertisements for tuxedo rentals on bulletin boards in the hallways of our school. In the ads, four guys in tuxedos squeezed in around one girl in a prom dress. She leaned against a surfboard. She laughed, as if she was having a blast, except that she was flipped upside down, headfirst toward the floor, and two of the boys each had a hand on one of her ankles. Her legs were in the air, spread open. At my high school, for many of the boys passing the poster and staring at the image, they soaked in the tired old trope that we were supposed to equate our prom with sex. But even more than that, we all saw something else shouting at us in the image. And even if many of the guys at my school wouldn't say it out loud, way too many of them shared this view: sex at prom—you are entitled to it.

Also, all the rest of the stuff that poster suggests? Yes, is definitely reinforcing the culture of misogyny.

And so a few of my friends and I talked about this subtext in the posters. But that's all we did. Talk about it. Until Mark spoke up.

"If we let these posters stand," he said, "we're endorsing the message they send."

Whoa. That socked us in our solar plexuses. He was right. Simply shaking our heads and doing nothing about it was hypocritical. It was cowardly. It was being complicit. And even more so, what did it say about us as friends to the girls we claimed we were friends with?

That we don't really have your back, even if we say we do?

So just like there was a Colin in middle school, there was a Mark in high school who stood up when something and someone (many someones) was wrong. But this time it was different. Mark, you might say, didn't just intervene and confront a bully—he didn't fight for someone, he fought with someone.

Even if she wasn't in the room.

Mark inspired us, rallied us, and at least a few of us knew what we had to do. We had to tear the posters down. We started with the posters on the first floor—doing it after school when the halls were much emptier.

And as you might have guessed, there were plenty of guys who laughed at us, who teased us in so many different ways that all seemed to say the same thing:

"Why are you making such a big deal out of nothing?"

"Don't take things so literally! It's supposed to be funny."

"Why do you have to take it all so seriously?"

All teasing, prodding questions that sound a lot like the kinds of things people say to protect boys and men when they actually do harm to girls and women:

"Oh, that's just boys being boys."

"But he has such a bright future ahead of him—don't ruin it for him."

"It's just a joke. Can't you take a joke?"

No, actually. No.

It isn't just a joke. (Yeah. See how that sounds now? Not so great.)

Language matters. Messaging matters. That poster mattered. The language we use, the media we stare at and consume—all of it affects our attitude. If we think trash talking women is no big deal but we do it all the time, maybe it's not just a joke anymore. Maybe it's how we actually feel. And what if we start to act on those feelings?

**DOING NOTHING
IS A BEHAVIOR.**

TAKE A GOOD, HARD LOOK IN THE MIRROR, BRENDAN, AND YOU'LL SEE YOUR PRIVILEGE OF NOT HAVING TO DO ANYTHING STARING RIGHT BACK AT YOU IN THE FACE.

Here is a terrifying statistic:

► One in three women in the United States of America are physically abused or sexually assaulted in their life.

In other words, there are more than 150 million women in the United States, and more than 50 million of them will experience the pain and trauma of assault (mostly by men). Way, way too many men in our country are cruel bullies (and worse!) to the women in their lives.

The language we use affects our attitude. And our attitudes affect our behavior.

Doing nothing is a behavior. So, if we didn't do something about the poster, we were still bullies. That's right. Take a good, hard look in the mirror, Brendan, and you'll see your privilege of not having to do anything staring right back at you in the face.

Yup. That's the kind of mirror we're getting at here: I can't speak truth to power unless I can first speak truth to myself.

So, I finally got what Mark was talking about. We had to stop the misogynistic poster from going unchecked or we would just be part of the problem. If we didn't act against that culture of misogyny, we were that culture of misogyny.

We men had to stand up to other men, to try to stop allowing misogyny to be woven so deeply and easily into our everyday conversations and environment. Because the terrible truth of that statistic isn't the result of a handful of brutally mean bullies. It's the result of an entire culture that protects and enables men at the cost of women's safety. It's other men protecting men who are bullies. It's men choosing to do nothing to stop the bullying or change the culture.

Rallying the guys together wasn't about Mark acting for someone else. It was about him working with someone else. Mark was being an ally to the girls who weren't even in our school. They couldn't see him, and they didn't need to. But the rest of us guys did.

Even though some guys had laughed at us and teased us for our anti-poster campaign, and someone ratted us out, we ended up having to speak to a teacher about the ads. He then had us sit down with the Dean of Students and a couple guidance counselors who, after our meeting, agreed to take down the rest of the posters. And once the posters came down, a lot more guys had to start talking about the misogynistic messaging in those posters, too.

No. We didn't "save the day." No. We were not heroes. We were trying to be allies. We started a conversation about misogynistic attitudes in our all-boys high school community—and that was at least something.

There are always too many bullies on the bus, in the hallway at school, in the locker room, on the soccer field, in the classroom— even behind the teacher's desk—and there are always kids feeling the pain these bullies inflict. They could use an ally. They could use a Colin or a Mark, but those people aren't always there and you can't always wait for someone else to do the work. But you're there.

So now what happens? Who will you be? The Brendan on the bus, Colin, or someone like Mark? Someone who understood that to be an ally isn't only about having the courage to challenge bullies. It's also knowing that sometimes doing nothing is as bad as sticking gum in someone's hair. It's not being afraid of working with others to change something, even if it's only the culture in your school.

You have to take a good look in the mirror and decide. Because it's your own face, dude.

TRAVEL LOGS OF A BLACK CARIBBEAN WOMAN: EMBRACING THE GLITCHES

SHAKIRAH BOURNE

In *The Matrix* movie, Neo is looking for answers because he has a niggling feeling that something is wrong with his world. He experiences "Glitches"—inexplicable errors in his reality. When he gets a message to "follow the white rabbit," he meets Morpheus, who gives him the choice to see the ugly truth, and Neo discovers he's been living in a simulated reality controlled by machines.

Morpheus was Black. Neo was white. And though race relations weren't relevant to the plot of the film, when Morpheus gives Neo the chance to remain ignorant of the realities of the world and keep his rose-tinted perspective of life, his privilege was clear—he got to choose.

So many people of color do not.

A key step to becoming an ally is empathy—opening your eyes to the reality of the less privileged and acknowledging that despite your best efforts, you may have implicit biases and prejudices.

These are travel logs of my physical and psychological journey to recognizing racism underneath the veil of pretense. A round trip from ignorance to awareness.

In the movie, when Neo moved toward implementing change, he encountered Agents, guardians of the matrix who defended the system against anyone who threatened to reveal the truth.

Beware, the agents that protect systemic racism in the real world may be operated by your sweet old neighbor who bakes you cookies, a beloved family member, or your closest friend.

And allies can be those who you least expect . . .

A KEY STEP TO BECOMING AN ALLY IS EMPATHY—OPENING YOUR EYES TO THE REALITY OF THE LESS PRIVILEGED AND ACKNOWLEDGING THAT DESPITE YOUR BEST EFFORTS, YOU MAY HAVE IMPLICIT BIASES AND PREJUDICES.

BARBADOS

To an outsider, Barbados is a picture of racial harmony. A place to vacation. Take long walks on white sand and have smiling locals serve you food and drink on the beach.

"Happy" is our brand.

People of all races greet each other on the street, mingle at restaurants, and apologize with a chuckle when our shopping carts accidentally bump in supermarket aisles.

A photographer could snap a photo at any minute and use it in a brochure.

Early on, someone tried to shatter my virtual reality. They told me Barbados is like a successful apartheid. Everyone lives in relative peace with each other, maintaining our matrix—our fragile dream world of civility. That there is no need for "Whites Only" signs to separate us. Everyone knows their place.

I dismissed that theory. Made excuses. I didn't want to disturb my bubble. Until I experienced my first Glitch.

BARBADOS, 1997

I was devastated when I found out I had gotten into one of the most prestigious high schools on the island. You see, I had heard stories about snobby rich students who ate sandwiches with knives and forks and turned their noses up at everything fun. I came from a poor family and thought I would be a fish out of water, a prime candidate for shunning.

It was a relief to discover this was not the case. Yes, most of my new classmates came from middle and upper class families, but we were all scared eleven-year-olds in new blue tunics and white-starched blouses, anxious about the new environment and desperate to make friends.

For the first time, I had white classmates. But though there had been no white kids at my elementary school in a working class community, I was no stranger to interacting with white people.

My mother was a waitress at a hotel, and as she was a single mother, my younger sister and I spent many a day playing by the pool with white kids from the US and UK while she finished her double shift.

At school, I quickly made friends with kids as weird as me, who invented nerdy songs and were obsessed with the Spice Girls. Though we all identified as Black, I was the only Barbadian-born member of the group. When the lunch bell rang, I noticed a large, white picnic bench under a few trees; it looked like a great place to eat my soggy tuna sandwiches.

"Not there, that's the white bench," an older student said. We were confused, until a few seconds later when a large group of white students squeezed themselves onto the bench.

They literally meant the *white* bench.

We laughed and shrugged it off. White people were the minority, so what if they felt more comfortable eating together? People gravitate toward the familiar, right?

One day we were let out of class early, and the white bench looked particularly inviting, an empty haven from the hot sun.

"Let's go sit on the white bench," I said, and we giggled at the thought of breaking the unofficial rule. The four of us ate our lunch at the bench, and when the bell rang we expected the white students to join us.

Except . . . they never came.

Soon we began to feel an angry heat that had nothing to do with the sun. The white students had gathered under a nearby tree, openly glaring at us. We squeezed closer together to show there was still enough room on the bench for everyone, but no one joined us. Their whispers floated in the wind, spooking away our appetites. Soon, we packed up our lunch and left.

We returned to our classroom in an uncomfortable silence, and then peeked over the balcony. Eventually, two white students approached the bench, and as if they telepathically indicated it was safe, everyone else followed. A few of them wiped the seat and my friends and I gave each other knowing looks.

"Maybe we left some crumbs behind," Marie said, the eternal optimist. This happens when you experience your first Glitch. It's easier to make excuses than to confront a hurtful reality. We brushed the incident aside and forgot all about it.

Years later I would relay this story to a friend, but then reassured her that the white kids in my class were nice. They never ate lunch on the white bench. They were allies. If any of them had been around that day, they would have sat next to us on that bench. Maybe their acceptance would have shown the other white kids that everyone was welcome to join us. We could have all exchanged soggy sandwiches, traded stories about teachers, and if they were up for it, belted out a few Spice Girl tunes.

Then my friend asked if I ever went to any of my white classmates' houses to hang out or was invited to their birthday parties . . . and I was silent.

BARBADOS, 2004

Growing up in a country that is majority Black is a privilege, especially for Black people. I had never been afraid to walk the streets because of the color of my skin. Our elected politicians are Black. Our newscasters are Black. Seeing a police officer coming toward me with a firm face only brings about fears of getting a parking ticket. I've never had to think about racially motivated violence—never saw a white police officer anywhere but on TV until I visited America as a teen. Since our independence from Britain, Black people have held most visible positions of power.

But if you take a closer look, you'll see that in a country that is 92% Black, the 3% of white people control the majority of the economic wealth, thanks to the continuously reaped benefits of the transatlantic slave trade and lingering effects of colonialism.

This became clear to me during an Economics lecture at college, when the class was divided into groups to analyze annual reports for some of the most profitable conglomerates on the island. Afterward, we came together to compare notes:

"Wait, that guy is on the board at this company, too."

"I have him, too!"

"And him as well!"

"Me, too!"

It was like we found Old White Dude bingo cards or had photocopied the board of directors with the same smiling white men for each annual report. It was an enlightening moment, like when you figure out the plot twist for a movie. The 3% may not be visible on local TV or in parliament, but they are present behind the scenes, holding the invisible economic power.

It was hard to ignore that Glitch. Not when the evidence was clear on satin-coated paper. So instead, we rationalized.

"They inherited these companies from family, what were they supposed to do? Refuse the business opportunity?"

"My mother works for this man and he treats his staff like family. They're putting food on hundreds of Barbadian tables."

"Black people need to stop being so frightened and take more risks in business."

The power of the machines is strong and we needed an ally then.

I wish a student had pointed out that the white people's wealth had been accumulated over several hundred years of slavery and exploitation of the blood, sweat, death, and little-mentioned innovations of our ancestors.

That the first formerly enslaved people allowed to own land on the island did so less than two-hundred years ago, and that one had to be a property owner to have the right to vote until 1950— approximately seventy years ago!

A WRITER FRIEND MENTIONED THAT HER GREAT-GREAT GRANDFATHER BOUGHT HER GREAT-GREAT GRANDMOTHER AT AN AUCTION.

Though it was an Economics class, I wish the professor would have recognized the relevance of our history, and highlighted that when slavery was abolished, the plantation owners—the predecessors of the smiling white men on the boards—were handsomely compensated, lining their pockets even further. That less than ninety years ago, Black people on the island rose up in rebellion due to dismal labor and social conditions, still dictated by the white elites, one hundred years after the abolition of slavery.

But no one spoke up. Instead, snippets of hard truths later told the story.

Before she passed, my grandmother, who had worked on a plantation, still became tongue-tied when I brought a white friend to meet her.

A writer friend mentioned that her great-great grandfather bought her great-great grandmother at an auction.

A colleague confided that the easiest way to get a bank loan for a new small business was to get any white man as a silent partner.

CONVERSATIONS ABOUT RACE AND INEQUALITY WILL NEVER BE COMFORTABLE TO HAVE, NO MATTER THE OCCASION.

I thought about these facts when I was trying to charm a wealthy white resident to invest in a film over dinner, and they mentioned that slavery was so long ago and Black people need to get over it.

I paused, the knife and fork hovering over my salmon. Sometimes when you experience a Glitch you make the excuse that the timing isn't right. Not over dinner. Not in a business setting. Not with a new acquaintance. But conversations about race and inequality will never be comfortable to have, no matter the occasion.

I wish that I was brave enough to speak out then. I wished I had witnessed more allies calling out friends and colleagues when they made ignorant statements, not with the intention to embarrass, but to educate.

I was scared. I didn't know how to tackle such a conversation. So instead, I continued to eat my meal, even though the perfectly-seasoned fish now had no taste.

EDINBURGH, SCOTLAND, 2010

For the first time, I was living in a country where I was in the minority. I went to a party with some other college students, including my classmate, Carolina, a Black woman from Portugal. She was one of the more mature students in my year, and I admired her confidence and her drive.

In a conversation at a party, I spoke about being accustomed to interacting with persons of various races and ethnicities, and that when I looked at my friends I didn't see white Greek, or white German, I saw quirky Sophia, and jovial Emily. Then I uttered the words, "I don't see color."

Everyone nodded, but Carolina took my hand, smiling. "Shakirah, of course you see color," she said. "If you didn't see color, you wouldn't see me. You wouldn't see yourself."

> **IF YOU DON'T SEE COLOR, YOU'RE ERASING OUR STRUGGLE, IGNORING OUR BATTLES.**

Though she said it in the gentlest way, shame rushed to my head. I opened my mouth to clarify I didn't mean it like that, but then realized I was making the same excuse white people made when they were called out for saying something ignorant. In that moment, instead of trying to justify my behavior, I had to accept my own problematic views and actions. I was basically giving every white person on that balcony permission to parrot such a problematic statement.

I know some people utter these words with the best intentions, but if you don't see color, then you don't see the discrimination forced upon millions of people. If you don't see color, you're erasing our struggle, ignoring our battles.

That phrase never left my lips again, and now I knew how to call out someone if they made the same ignorant statement.

I think about my words every time I have to correct some well-meaning white person who claims they don't discriminate against any skin color; black, purple, or blue, as if millions of purple people have died fighting for basic human rights, or Smurfs revolted on sugar plantations. I replay that moment at the party all the time, and get ashamed all over again. I'm grateful that Carolina was there to educate me. It's hard to call out someone in public, especially people from your own community.

Years later, I messaged Carolina and thanked her, since I had only given a stiff nod at the time. She didn't remember saying it. Small moments of speaking out can have life-changing, perspective-altering effects on others, even if they seem insignificant to you.

EDINBURGH, SCOTLAND, 2011

I was always surrounded by friends on campus, but when I enrolled in a writing course at another college, twice a week I caught the bus by myself. In those rare moments that I was alone, I stared at my reflection in the bus window and was reminded that I was a Black girl with long dreadlocks in a majority white country.

One day, I realized that the seat next to me remained vacant for a very long time. The route began near my campus and so it was often almost empty when I boarded. But by the time we reached the city center, there was usually standing room only.

Soon I noticed that people would only sit next to me when the seat was one of the last remaining. I chided myself for being paranoid. Creating an unnecessary Glitch in the matrix.

But for fun, I created a game—Let's See When Someone Sits Next to Me. I sat near the front, and made myself as small as possible. Week after week, my seat would be one of the last to be filled. I moved positions, sitting at the front, middle, back of the bus—it changed nothing.

I kept my face turned to the window to seem as nonthreatening as possible, but it didn't help. One time, the bus almost made it all the way to the city center, with some passengers even choosing to stand, before I felt a presence easing into the seat beside me. Soon, I started to regret these journeys to the city alone, even as I tried to find humor in my game.

One week, just when my game was about to begin, a young white woman slid into the seat beside me. I actually jumped, then tried not to move in case I scared her away. I couldn't believe it; there were still prime window seats available!

She didn't take notice of me at all—no overly polite nods, no forced half-smiles, no hesitation before sitting. She spent most of the time on her phone. I have never felt so grateful to be unnoticeable.

AN ALLY HAS TO DO CONSTANT SELF-INTERROGATION BECAUSE IT'S HARD TO CORRECT A BIAS THAT YOU DON'T KNOW EXISTS.

When she got off the bus, I wanted to wave goodbye. She'd never know how much her short companionship meant to me.

How could she? Until then, when I was struggling to hold back tears while she sat there, I had no idea how much it hurt to play the game.

I don't believe every single person who didn't sit next to me was racist. Some of them may have considered themselves to be allies to marginalized communities, but an ally has to do constant self-interrogation because it's hard to correct a bias that you don't know exists.

I don't expect anyone else would be playing Let's See When Someone Sits Next to Me. But whenever I board a bus overseas, I take a seat next to a person of color, especially if their face is turned toward the window, just in case.

PHILADELPHIA, 2012

One of my aunts—who had never stepped foot off the island— would frown while watching US news reports and tut, "why are African Americans so angry?" She'd complain about the gangsters and drug addicts creating bad neighborhoods, and giving Black people a bad reputation. Unfortunately, many Caribbean people, who thought themselves superior to the "violent" African Americans portrayed on TV, shared her sentiments. Sometimes Black people can be unknowing Agents of the system.

I was excited about this trip to Philadelphia to visit my friend Marie from the Bahamas, who was now a student at college.

Marie and I were walking downtown when at least ten police cars sped past, lights and sirens blaring. They screeched and made U-turns on the other side of the road, and officers jumped out, guns armed and ready. I felt like a bystander in one of those cop shows on TV. Then, four of the police officers grabbed two young Black men and shoved them onto the ground.

Marie and I stopped, and stepped under a store awning to avoid the other pedestrians, who didn't break stride.

It seemed so unnecessary to have all these police officers here, just to arrest two men, so I was convinced there was a bigger catastrophe at hand. It probably wasn't the wisest decision to stay; if there was a bomb we would have been wiped away, but we were rooted to the spot.

Suddenly, the demeanor of all the officers changed. They put away their guns, leaned against cars, and laughed. If I were a cartoon character my mouth would have fallen onto the floor. Marie and I looked on in confusion as the police officers removed the handcuffs on the two men, and then drove off.

We went to see if the men were okay and found out what happened. The police officers were looking for thieves who had robbed a nearby store. They thought that the young Black men fit the description of the suspects, but then got a call that the actual perpetrators were apprehended.

The boys shrugged.

Shrugged! Like if the police had asked them for directions instead of planting their bodies into the ground like seeds.

"Why aren't you more upset?" I asked, looking at them in disbelief.

"This happens all the time."

They thanked us for staying, and then walked away. We stood there, gaping at their backs, until they disappeared into the flood of pedestrians, who still had not paused. I thought about my aunt shaking her head, and frowning at the television, and knew I needed to face reality.

I had been in America for two days, and I was angry, too.

NEW YORK, 2012

A few days after the incident in Philadelphia, I packed my suitcase and headed to the Big Apple. You know those movies where the country girl moves to the city, and we see her head sticking out of a cab, gaping up at skyscrapers that kissed clouds? That was me. I had a blast exploring Times Square and Broadway.

But then reality kicked in—the noise and chaos, and my expressions of wonder were replaced by fear when I had to unravel the subway and train system, attempting to make my way to a friend in the neighboring state of New Jersey.

Thankfully, I found my way to the correct station in suburban New Jersey. The worst part of the journey was over. According to her directions, all I had to do now was get a taxi from the station to her apartment, seven minutes away.

Turns out it was easier for me to navigate the subway than it was to get a taxi.

There was a line of cabs with drivers, but when I went to give the first one the address, he said he wasn't working.

Neither was the cab behind him.

Or the next.

I held on to the I ♥ NY hat I had just bought in Times Square, looked up at the darkening sky, and tried not to panic. But this wasn't New York. There were no taxis zipping up and down every half-second. There was only this bunch of defunct taxis—a cab graveyard with drivers paying respects in the front seats.

I kept walking down the line. No. No. No. Some didn't speak; they just dismissed me with a wave of their hand. Some avoided my question and stared down at newspapers.

Finally, when I was about to give up, a driver waved me over.

Cautiously, I leaned over when I got close. "Hello, are you working?"

"Yes, hop in. I'll take you," he responded.

I was relieved. I relaxed in the back seat, finally able to admire the quiet neighborhood now that I was safe.

"Ignore them," the driver said, breaking the silence. "They're idiots."

"Who?" I replied, confused.

"The other drivers."

"Oh no, they weren't working," I said, correcting him.

"Oh, they were working!" he exclaimed.

Now I was more confused. "So why didn't they want to take me?"

I remember the driver looking into the rear-view mirror. He adjusted it; as though he wanted to see me clearly, make sure that he wasn't making a mistake.

"Because you're Black!" he yelled. My eyes widened in shock, and a little embarrassment to be honest. It was only then I realized that he was Black, too, and the other taxi drivers had been of other races. I might as well have been wearing Barbados's national costume because it was clear I was an outsider and didn't understand the dynamics of this matrix. But I had enough. That Black taxi driver didn't know it, but he pushed me down the rabbit hole, and I had a clear view of harsh reality.

After the shock wore off, I became angry. Again. It was 2012. Barack Obama—the first Black president of the United States—had just been elected for a second term. People were celebrating the accomplishment as evidence that racism no longer existed in the country.

Yet, if it weren't for a taxi-man, who didn't see me as a Bajan, Caribbean, African, or African American, but as a fellow Black person in need of assistance, I would have been stranded at an empty station in New Jersey.

BARBADOS, 2020

With the rise of the Black Lives Matter movement in the US, it became harder for the world to maintain the matrix. That movement has spread across the globe, impacting even the shores of Barbados, finally disrupting the mirage and exposing wounds that never had the space to heal.

When Barbadians witnessed protesters in the US topple statues of American slaveowners and Confederate monuments, eyes inevitably turned to the bronze statue of British Admiral Lord Nelson, a keen supporter of the transatlantic slave trade and the British empire, that had been towering in the middle of the city center in our renamed National Heroes Square since 1813. There had been a resolution in the 1990s to have this statue removed, followed by decades of sporadic debate, but it was only after a local Black Lives Matter protest and a #NelsonMustGo petition, that the government made an incredible announcement: Nelson was coming down.

Suddenly, the statue, which is located in an area not often frequented by upper classes of society, became an important symbol of white Barbadian history. Several white Bajans took to social media to denounce the relocation of the statue to the museum since it would be "erasing our history." One white business owner insisted that she was tired of hearing about racism and seeing hate toward white people, especially in the height of tourist season. She insisted that "Blacks get rid of the chip on their shoulder to move forward."

Another comment that received support from their community came from a white man who claimed that Barbados's independence from Britain was the most racist act, one that lowered the standard of living on the island, and moving the Nelson statue was another racist action that would come at a high cost.

Suddenly the mirage of racial harmony was broken. The matrix was temporarily shut down and #ScreenshotARacist became a local social media campaign.

Expletives were shared. Families divided. Friendships broken. Businesses canceled. Employees fired. Racists went back into hiding. People went back to living.

But one thing was clear: it took more than thirty years to remove the statue, a symbol of our colonial past, but it will take much longer to remove the lingering stench of racism and segregation on the island. We can no longer pretend it does not exist.

There's so much more I want to talk about—why I sometimes feel sad when I visit museums since I'm reminded that my own history

> **I AM UNCOMFORTABLE WITH PLANTATIONS WHO GIVE GUIDED TOURS WITHOUT MENTIONING THEIR COLONIAL AND SLAVE-OWNING PAST, AND CROC-WEARING TOURISTS TRAMPLE ON THE UNMARKED GRAVES OF THE ENSLAVED TO SAMPLE RUM.**

has been destroyed. Why I got offended when a white man shared a photo from 1900s Barbados and lamented about the "good ole days," a time when my ancestors were disenfranchised of basic human rights. Why I am uncomfortable with plantations who give guided tours without mentioning their colonial and slave-owning past, and Croc-wearing tourists trample on the unmarked graves of the enslaved to sample rum. But there is no word count large enough to cover all the overt and subtle prejudices faced by Black people every single day.

I needed allies who could disrupt the system so many times, even when I didn't know it. A white student could have joined us on that white bench. Someone could have given pseudo-intellectual Economics students a history lesson and called us out on our ignorant statements, just like Carolina did at the party. More strangers could have sat next to me on the bus . . .

Allyship is a never-ending journey. I have to actively work toward recognizing signs of subtle racism, and the mechanics of systemic racism that continues to manifest itself in multiple forms to disenfranchise marginalized people around the world. I still make mistakes and have to be educated. But choosing to be an ally is to continuously listen, learn, improve, question, and then reeducate others, and always, always paying attention to the Glitches.

STUTTER BUDDY

DERICK BROOKS

I didn't realize it's not always that simple until I met *Lauren*.

She's the smartest, coolest, funniest person I know.

But also, she stutters.

*When it happens it's like she's blocked
by a wall that only exists for her.*

She can't jump over it.

She can't go around it.

Sometimes she can find a different path.

Sometimes she can press into it.

Either way she might run into it again.

It makes some people uncomfortable,
but that's on them.

I think she's cool.

Choosing to tell people about her
stutter can be exhausting.

She doesn't do it to
make them feel better.

She does it to take care of herself, because
her thoughts and feelings are important.

And I promise you . . .

It's worth the wait.

9

THE UNSAFE SPACE

ADIBA JAIGIRDAR

For most of my life, I've lived in Ireland, a country that hasn't always been super progressive. In the last few years it has come leaps and bounds in terms of progress, but when me and my friends were teenagers, we didn't have ways to learn about things like feminism. In school, we didn't even learn about the suffragettes and women's fight for the right to vote. In terms of issues of race, the most we ever learned was the American civil rights movement. Which—while an incredibly important facet of history—wasn't our country's (or even our continent's) history with racism. And it was never taught in a way that felt relatable to our present day.

And that's probably why college, and the opportunity to finally have language and space to talk about these ideas, felt like a profound time in our lives.

After I finished college, me and a few of my friends decided we needed to create a similar space where we would be able to freely explore our ideas. Where we could engage in important discourse about topics and values that were important to us. We were all women from various backgrounds, and in our time in college many of us had had our first taste of studying feminism.

For many of us, it was our first opportunity to read works by famous feminists; the ones who were, and continue to be,

essential to the feminist movement. Women like bell hooks, Judith Butler, Angela Davis; feminists who created revolutionary change and are still at the forefront of change today. So, we wanted to create a specifically feminist space.

We worked together on a website, a magazine, a podcast; all interconnected under one title. We were hopeful and excited to connect with the world around us, now that we were fresh out of college and had bright new ideas.

We wanted to create a community of women from diverse backgrounds. To create dialogue that felt relevant to women like us; to be accessible and inclusive. What we really wanted, I think, was to create something that we never had; both the knowledge we didn't have access to until we went to college, and a safe space to discuss things relevant to us. One of the key points in our mission statement even detailed one of our main goals as "to be inclusive of minority voices who are often unheard in popular media."

There were four people in our core group: Sarah, Abigail, Nathalie, and me. We'd all known each other since school and kept up that friendship even when we went our different ways afterwards. We were bonded by our love of creativity, and of writing.

Everything started off really well, and we were vibing off of each other. But it wasn't long before tension started filtering into this space that was supposed to be inclusive. Every time we talked about issues concerning race, I became deeply aware of the fact that I was both the only woman of color in our core group, and the only Muslim woman.

This wasn't unusual in my experience. During most of my time in college, I was the only Muslim or person of color in lecture halls full of hundreds of people. I had learned that there were often

times when people would say racist and Islamophobic things, and I learned to keep my mouth shut unless I wanted to constantly be arguing with near strangers and educating them in my daily life.

But in this space, I had expected something different.

> **INSTEAD OF ENCOURAGING THE SHARING OF DIVERSE PERSPECTIVES, I FOUND MY VOICE BEING SHUT DOWN OVER AND OVER AGAIN.**

These weren't near strangers, they were my friends. People who had known me for most of my life. More importantly, they wanted to create a space for all women. But I became aware of being the only Muslim woman of color because the space we created didn't cater to me. Instead of encouraging the sharing of diverse perspectives, I found my voice being shut down over and over again.

The first time this registered in my mind was during a podcast recording session when we discussed one of the few Disney movies with a character of color: *Moana*. At first, our conversation was thriving. That was until Sarah started talking about class, suggesting that she was disappointed to see yet another movie where the princess was from a higher class, as Moana is the chief's daughter.

I pointed out that class seemed to work very differently in Moana's island community. Instead of the kings, queens, princes, and princesses we had seen in most Disney Princess movies, Moana's island seemed to be about community and supporting each other. Moana's placement as a "princess" seemed more about making her part of Disney's "princess line," rather than an actual role in her community. Instead of engaging with what I brought up, Sarah claimed that she still believed Moana to be extremely privileged, like other Disney princesses. She couldn't see the difference between the white European princesses in other Disney movies and Moana's Polynesian community. We moved on from the conversation swiftly to keep the podcast engaging, but I remember feeling unsettled as the conversation carried on.

Later on, after all the recording equipment had been put away, we naturally fell back into discussing *Moana* once more. This time, Sarah, Nathalie, and Abigail all praised the movie for not giving Moana a love interest. I listened to their discussion before adding my own opposing view: I thought it was great to see more media where women didn't have love interests, and romance wasn't the focus. But it was frustrating that it was so often women of color in media who didn't have love interests, and are presented like we're supposed to be strong. We often don't get portrayed as vulnerable people who are loved and cared for by a love interest.

I had hoped that we could speak about how love, romance, and desirability can look very different for white women vs. women of color. Instead, all my friends stared back at me with question marks on their faces, like they couldn't even fathom the idea of what I had just said.

"How would Moana even have had a love interest?" Sarah asked. "Maui is way too old for her." I couldn't understand how that was the only thing Sarah took away from what I had said, but I was feeling deeply unsettled once more.

In another instance, Sarah shared an article in our group chat that was rife with Islamophobia. The article, written by a white non-Muslim woman presented Muslims, specifically prominent Muslim women of color, as anti-feminist for not speaking enough on issues of veiling and women who do not want to veil.

I wasn't unused to dealing with this kind of Islamophobia. My experience of existing as a Muslim woman of color had consisted of people who did not know the first thing about being Muslim telling me that my religion must oppress me. Of people participating in debates and discussions about women like me, and about whether we should be allowed to veil or not—debates and discussions where Muslim women, and specifically Muslim hijabis, were almost never present or given a voice. This was simply another instance of having my voice as a Muslim woman erased. But this time, I hadn't expected it. I hadn't expected it from this space, meant to be inclusive and safe. From these friends, meant to be feminists and allies.

When I brought up the point that what is anti-feminist is yet another non-Muslim voice on Muslim women's issues, which tore down Muslim women of color, Sarah immediately became defensive.

She said that everyone should know that whenever she shared an article with us, it wasn't because she agreed with it, it's because she hoped it would "elicit discussion." But of course, nobody was having discussions about whether women like Sarah—white, atheist, and brought up in a Catholic household—should be able to choose what she wanted to wear. Nobody was telling her that her religion or beliefs were inherently oppressive.

But as a Muslim woman, I had to deal with Islamophobia every single day. And I couldn't believe that even in what was supposed to be a "safe space," and "feminist space," women like me were just a point of discussion rather than reality.

A few weeks later, someone changed the topic to something completely unrelated, as if everything I had said about Islamophobia was making them uncomfortable.

The message to me was clear: nobody would speak up for me.

> I COULDN'T BELIEVE THAT EVEN IN WHAT WAS SUPPOSED TO BE A "SAFE SPACE," AND "FEMINIST SPACE," WOMEN LIKE ME WERE JUST A POINT OF DISCUSSION RATHER THAN REALITY.

Nobody would apologize for what had been said and done. But I was expected to move on.

I secretly hoped that despite their silence, my friends had taken something away. That next time something might be different. It wasn't long before I was proven wrong.

It was the summer that the first *Wonder Woman* film was due to be released, and everybody was excited. After years of superhero movies with male leads, we were finally getting a major female lead. And it was Wonder Woman, someone who stood for justice!

Except there were many people uncomfortable with the star of the movie being Gal Gadot: a woman who has been criticized for her pro–Israeli Defense Force stance, for her participation as a soldier in the IDF, and her continued support of the IDF during the Israeli occupation of Palestine.

I had hoped that everybody in our group had simply missed all the criticism on social media, and after I told them a little bit about it, we would be able to discuss how the actress of a character meant to stand for justice, seems to support this injustice. Instead, Sarah became dismissive once more.

According to her, it was anti-feminist to say that Gal Gadot's involvement with the IDF was a more pressing issue. It was an attempt at stifling the important discussion of the all-women *Wonder Woman* screenings that were plastered across social media.

> **THEY WANTED TO TALK ABOUT WOMEN OF COLOR WITHOUT LISTENING TO US, WITHOUT VALUING US. WITHOUT THINKING ABOUT US AS ACTUAL HUMAN BEINGS. WE EXISTED WHEN WE AGREED WITH THEIR POINTS OR OPINIONS, BUT IF WE DIDN'T, SOMEHOW THAT MADE US "ANTI-FEMINIST."**

Once more, I waited for someone—anyone—to speak up. Though I knew it was useless. I was exhausted from having these discussions about the existence of women like me. I had nothing more to say, especially when nobody else was willing to help, or listen to me.

A few weeks later, Abigail dismissively told me that she was glad she never got involved in those arguments between me and Sarah. As if we were children arguing over ice-cream flavors. I was both shocked and disappointed that someone who called herself a feminist, and an intersectional one no less, could be so dismissive.

But I had learned by now that speaking up in this space that I had helped create, speaking about my experiences, was completely devalued by people who I had thought of as friends.

Instead of stopping for a moment and engaging with the idea that my lived experience as a Muslim woman of color means that I have things to add to the conversation, every time I suggested an opposing point I was shut down. In many ways, my "inclusive," "intersectional," "feminist" friends were doing exactly what the non-Muslim woman writing the article on veiling had done. They wanted to talk about women of color without listening to us, without valuing us. Without thinking about us as actual human beings. We existed when we agreed with their points or opinions, but if we didn't, somehow that made us "anti-feminist."

Intersectionality can be defined as an understanding that all parts of our identity are interconnected and can't be separated. All of us are a mixture of many different identities. As a Muslim, able-bodied, cis woman of color my lived experience will be different from an able-bodied cis white Catholic woman. And both of our experiences will also be different from a white trans disabled person.

There are endless intersections, and none of us is defined by a singular part of our identity. We all have different experiences of the world, and in the kind of feminist space we wanted to create, intersectionality should have led to great conversation. Instead, it led to erasure and prejudice.

So much of the building of that space felt fake, like a performance. Everybody knew to use the right words, but there was no action that actually helped to create a safe or inclusive space. We often refer to this as performative allyship. When people speak about showing support or solidarity to marginalized groups but without any real action or follow-through. It's done for the sake of a pat on the back, to show that they are a good person or a good ally. But it does little to nothing to help marginalized groups or people. Often, it may end up harming them.

I did not find any allies in that space, which turned out to be toxic to people of color.

I quit before even a year was up, unable to cope with constantly having my voice put down.

After I left, and my mental health significantly improved, I found space to begin working on fiction that featured Muslim women of color. I found a way to give voice to people like me, maybe because that experience and countless others kept telling me that my voice, and my identity, didn't have any value. I wanted to prove to myself and to others that it does.

A few months after I had made the decision to quit, citing my own work and mental health as reasons for quitting (they held some truth, but were certainly not the main reason), I finally shared with a friend from that group why I had made the decision to leave.

Me and Nathalie had been close long before we started this website. We would meet up often in each other's places—from doing homework together when we were teens, to just finding time to hang out and talk as adults.

During one of these meet-ups at her house, we both shared how we had been frustrated by that group for various reasons.

Emboldened by our shared frustrations, I began to recount each incident where I was shut down from speaking, where I felt like my experience and voice were devalued, along with how bearing with the silence of people like her and everybody else on our team was taking a toll on me.

Nathalie listened to me with rapt attention, her expression becoming more and more shocked with every single thing I told her. Like she had really never noticed any of these things that had happened right in front of her face. I wasn't sure whether to laugh or cry at the fact that micro- and macro-aggressive incidences which would stay with me probably for the rest of my life were nothing but a blip on the memory of my white "feminist" friends.

As I finished up my story about how white feminists ran me out of a website that I, myself, cofounded, Nathalie did the most peculiar thing.

She began crying.

At first, I could only blink at her in confusion. Then, she started berating herself.

How could she not
have seen all of
this was going on?

How could I have
been dealing with all of
this while she watched
on, unaware?

INSTEAD OF SPENDING TIME
TALKING ABOUT THE RACISM
AND ISLAMOPHOBIA I HAD
DEALT WITH, THE REST OF
OUR TIME TOGETHER WAS
SPENT WITH ME TRYING
TO COMFORT AND
REASSURE.

What a bad friend she was for
not catching on earlier.

What a bad feminist she was, for not speaking up about all of
this while it was happening.

And on, and on, and on . . . Instead of spending time talking
about the racism and Islamophobia I had dealt with, the rest
of our time together was spent with me trying to comfort and
reassure. Telling her that she wasn't the only one who missed
all of this, there were other people there, too. That she shouldn't
beat herself up.

Later, when I was alone once more, I felt even worse off than
before I had unloaded everything. I felt exhausted, and I wasn't
even sure why.

In recent years, I've had more time to evaluate the past, and to
think about how we view ourselves vs. how we present ourselves.
What spaces we occupy as allies and how we occupy those
spaces.

At the time when I approached Nathalie to tell her about my
experiences, what would have happened if she hadn't begun to
cry? If, instead of berating herself for everything she had done
wrong or not noticed, or not done enough of, she had given me
the space to explore and delve into what had happened to me?
I would have left her that day feeling less tired. It would have

probably taken me far less time to finally be able to speak about these kinds of experiences with people again.

I chose to put aside my own needs and make Nathalie feel better. But in reality, I wasn't really given a choice. I was either going to be the horrible person kicking her friend when she was down, or I was going to be the good friend who didn't make someone feel worse after they broke down into tears.

So, I chose to put aside my feelings and my needs and focus on comforting her about the racism I had faced.

It sounds a little ridiculous to write it out. But this happens, time and again. All my friends in that group continuously centered themselves. It didn't matter when they had little to no knowledge or experience about what they were speaking about, it didn't matter when it was about me sharing my traumatic experience . . . they put themselves and their thoughts and feelings at the center. And I was the one who felt devalued, dismissed, and hurt. Over and over again.

Though I never officially "broke off" any friendships, I definitely felt a shift in how I thought of all of these women, who I once considered my close friends and allies. A shift that led to most of these friendships becoming unsalvageable.

These kinds of situations are going to continue to happen unless as allies we learn how to decenter ourselves and prioritize the feelings and experiences of those who need our allyship. When we do that, we allow marginalized people to feel like they're being listened to, to feel that their experiences are valid.

And when we don't, we continue to make them feel invalidated, dehumanized, and keep causing them harm.

There are a lot of reasons why our first instinct in the face of situations like this is to center our own voices and our own experiences.

We are intimately familiar with ourselves and our experience of the world, in a way that we will never be with people who we don't share a marginalization with. We might never understand the experience that they had; because we have not experienced the life that they have. Still, we've been taught that we must be empathetic—we have to relate other people's experiences to ours.

But the simple fact of the matter is that we can't always be empathetic. A lot of the time we simply can't relate other people's experience to ours. It's impossible. My white non-Muslim friend can never understand what it's like to exist in this world as a Muslim woman of color; all of the racism and microaggression I have to face day in and day out.

I also think there's a lot of discomfort when it comes to examining how we, as allies, can contribute to harm. Or where our own ignorance is. So many of us are always striving for perfect, and in the world that we live in there's this idea that if you're "problematic" you're a bad person.

But of course, we're all learning and growing. There have been times when I was ignorant of something and centered my own feelings and experience when the focus should have been on someone else. But most of us come to allyship with zero knowledge and experience, and it's our responsibility to fill in the gaps in our knowledge.

To suddenly learn that despite what you believe yourself to be—an ally, a feminist, whatever else—you somehow participated in hurting someone else; in letting your ignorance get the best of you . . . that can be difficult to face.

A lot of the time when this happens, we choose the easy route. We center ourselves and berate ourselves for not doing more.

But that's not actually the important thing. Our feelings are not

> **MOST OF US COME TO ALLYSHIP WITH ZERO KNOWLEDGE AND EXPERIENCE, AND IT'S OUR RESPONSIBILITY TO FILL IN THE GAPS IN OUR KNOWLEDGE.**

at the center of this situation. Of course, we should take from every experience and use it as an opportunity to learn; but to do that we have to actually engage with what we've done wrong, and listen to marginalized people.

Here are some things you can do to work on decentering yourself as an ally:

Listen to the person or group that you're an ally of. I imagine how things would have been different if when Sarah shared that extremely Islamophobic article everyone had reacted differently. Sarah could have listened to my perspective about how this article was Islamophobic and it wasn't okay to share something like that completely unprompted in a group that was supposed to be inclusive to marginalized identities and expect it to start conversation. She could have apologized for not thinking about how it must be difficult to have to deal with Islamophobia every day in all facets of life, and then to face it here, too, where I didn't expect it. Together, we could have all come up with a way to share articles like that in specific spaces with content warnings so everybody can choose how they interact with it or if they want to interact with it at all.

Prioritize their feelings over yours. If Nathalie didn't start talking about her guilt and her discomfort and how my trauma made her feel bad, I think I would have felt a lot better about the situation, instead of carrying around hurt and trauma for many years afterward. I wouldn't have felt horrible and empty, the way I

had when I left her house that day. Instead, I would have felt supported, listened to. I would have felt like, even if nobody else in that group had valued me and my perspective, Nathalie did. She may not have taken action before, but she was growing and learning and being a good ally and friend. And if something like this happened again, I would have felt comfortable confiding in her without wondering if she was going to make my trauma and hurt about her once more.

Act according to their needs. I often think about what I needed during the months when we worked on this website. I needed my friends to listen to me. I needed them to understand that my life as a Muslim woman of color was different from theirs. And that my perspective was different because of my experiences.

I needed my friends to support me when I felt like I had to defend my religion, and I needed them to understand that just because what was most important to me didn't match up with their feminism, it didn't make me anti-feminist. I needed much more than their silence. I needed them to act exactly as our mission statement presented us: inclusive, intersectional, and creating a space for discussion. But I didn't get any of that. Maybe if I had we would have achieved what we had set out to do. Or at least I would have left feeling better about who I was, about feminism, and about my friends.

Decentering ourselves is not always easy and might need a little bit of work. You might not get it right from the beginning, but it's worth it to keep trying. To be true allies, we have to decenter ourselves. Because it's only when we learn to decenter ourselves that we can properly center the people who need our allyship.

10

DISMANTLING JUDGMENT

LIZZIE HUXLEY-JONES

I've had many seizures in public.

One time, I crossed a busy London road with my partner Tim, only to keel over as my feet hit the pavement on the other side. A passerby whipped the coats off her children as well as her own, placing them around my body like a shield against the world.

Another time, I stumbled bleary-eyed out of a movie theater, having witnessed a particularly flashy scene there had been no warnings about. Everything went black, but as I began to wake up, my ears filled with jauntily played horns and drums. Circus music promoting a film I can no longer remember. The sparkling star pattern of the faux marble floor reflected on the lobby ceiling.

Those are some of the many times my partner has been there for and, crucially, are the ones people could see.

We call disabilities that are not easily visible "invisible disabilities." To the untrained eye a person might look completely fine, but may be struggling with a mental, physical, or neurological condition that impacts how they process, move, and interact with the world. This can make accessing support and asking for help much more difficult.

When you have a brain like mine, one that is prone to short-circuiting in hidden ways, navigating the world can be a difficult, sometimes dangerous, experience.

The year before the COVID-19 pandemic, I developed an orange-size cyst on my right ovary that kept bursting thanks to untreated endometriosis—we affectionately named him Drippy. Managing pain took over my life, even more than it had before, and I mostly stayed home, grasping little moments of independence when I had energy, while we waited six months for a surgery to sort everything out.

> WHEN YOU HAVE A BRAIN LIKE MINE, ONE THAT IS PRONE TO SHORT-CIRCUITING IN HIDDEN WAYS, NAVIGATING THE WORLD CAN BE A DIFFICULT, SOMETIMES DANGEROUS, EXPERIENCE.

Just before Drippy's arrival, a special interest in musical theater had unleashed itself with full force. This meant I had been sitting on an unsated desire to see a really good showstopping number with the West End only a twenty-minute train ride from my house, and limited at-home outlets to distract me from mounting an expedition. With support from my friends and Tim, I had managed to see *Come From Away* in September, and I had tickets to see *Dear Evan Hansen* in November when it opened in London. While I wouldn't rank *Evan* as a favorite musical, "Waving Through a Window" had become a bit of an anthem for me. I would belt it out as I hobbled around my tiny flat, clutching onto my protruding belly like a heavily pregnant person. I was told in October that my surgery would be happening in November, and the possibility of not being able to go made me want to go even more.

Luckily, my surgery was scheduled for after the night we had tickets, so I was all clear to go have a fun night out with my friend Lauren. That morning, I felt a bit strange—a little off-color in a way I couldn't work out—but as this ranked fairly low compared to the myriad ways I'd felt for six months, I decided to go. I left the house armored in an enormous fluffy pink coat and luminous yellow plaid dress, channeling Cher Horowitz energy.

We had a really nice time, and I cried my eyes out—because I will always cry at any piece of slightly emotive theater. It was only as I boarded the train at London Bridge that a familiar strangeness hit me. A seizure was coming.

I have two main types of seizure. One is essentially a jazzed-up faint and looks like a classic convulsion, the kind I had in those stories at the beginning. If not enough blood is getting to my head or I'm too hot, down I go. Over time, these have gotten easier to manage—you'll never see me without a huge bottle of water and an emergency salty snack pack.

The other is a kind of absence, heralded by a collection of odd sensations that we call an aura (which, a little confusingly, is technically a conscious seizure of its own). I will smell smoke that's not there, my teeth and jaw ache, and my body feels like it's rising, like I'm on a roller coaster going down the big drop. My neurologist and I think they're linked to how my autistic wiring processes overstimulation and stress, which makes them tricky to predict and prevent. My partner says that I look like I've powered down, and in a sense I have—I often don't know they've happened, the only sign being my little dog sitting in my lap, licking my face as I come around. But as I get closer to my brain rebooting like an ancient PC, I get clumsy and my words slur. I look drunk. And when the seizure is over, sometimes I can't speak at all.

Imaginary smoke filled the air around me and my heart started racing, thick heavy palpitations that I could hear in my ears. I slipped out of my coat, worried that I was unknowingly overheating, as autism means I lack interoception, the body's sixth sense, so can never tell if I'm too hot or cold. My fingers fumbled over my phone screen, writing "I feel strange" over to Tim, trying to remember how to tell him what was happening through the panic. What if this was a convulsion? What if my cyst burst again? What if I missed my stop?

A few years ago, I would go wandering, unknowingly having a seizure the whole time. My brain would usually autopilot me to safety and I would wake up in cafés or bookstores. My train was halfway to my home station. I had to hold on for another ten minutes. If I didn't, I'd miss my stop, ending up at the airport or the seaside where the train terminated.

Tim tried to keep me present by telling me about the new headphones he'd bought, but the nausea started to set in. My tongue felt huge in my mouth, an alien body part. I started to cry as my head twitched. This was definitely an aura. Blackout was getting closer.

I took a deep breath. Stay awake, I begged, running my fingers through my furry coat. My terrified reflection mirrored on the window, lit against the darkness outside. I tried to speak, but the swollen tongue that both was and wasn't mine wouldn't obey. A small moan poured out of me, words collapsed into a slick of noise, and I began to cry harder.

Another breath. I looked down at my phone, and pulled up the

THE LOOK IS AN ACT OF
JUDGMENT, WHEN WHAT YOU'RE
SEEING DOESN'T MATCH UP
WITH YOUR EXPECTATIONS, OR
EXPERIENCE TELLS YOU
SOMETHING STRANGE IS
HAPPENING. IT HAPPENS WHEN
PEOPLE ARE UNEQUIPPED,
NERVOUS, OR UNFAMILIAR WITH
A RANGE OF EXPERIENCES.

notes app. If I could catch someone's attention, I could show them a note on there that would explain I needed help. There weren't many people in the carriage around me. After wiping away tears and possible eyeliner trails, I turned my head to each of them in turn, hoping desperately to catch their eye. I did, a few times. And they all either looked away, or gave me The Look.

I find both reading and recognizing faces quite difficult—I've mistaken perfect strangers for my best friends just because they shared similar approximate outlines—but I know The Look a mile off. It's the moment that a person looks at you, sees something they think is strange, and so turn themselves away. It lightning-flashes over their features, and then they are gone before I can protest.

I've been seeing The Look since I was a child. At tweenage sleepovers where I couldn't handle the noise and asked if I could call my mum and go home. At a nice pub when, gathered with a lot of new people plus an ex, my arm wouldn't stop tremoring and these relative strangers kept glancing at me as I held tight onto my wrist, willing my body to stop rebelling. The Look is an act of judgment, when what you're seeing doesn't match up with your expectations, or experience tells you something strange is happening. It happens when people are unequipped, nervous, or unfamiliar with a range of experiences.

I needed help that day on the train. I was scared. I just needed someone to reach out and ask if I was okay. But they didn't. Somehow, I managed to stumble off the train at my stop with all my things, and waited in the ice-cold air for Tim to find me on the platform. No one there asked if I was okay either.

You might be surprised by this, but I don't blame people for The Look, or for their inaction. I know that people took one look at my outfit, my tears, and the phone clutched in my hand and thought either that I was too drunk or just-dumped or just a "hysterical woman." This makes me a little sad because I think even if I was any of the above, I still deserved compassion from strangers. The point is, I suppose, that they didn't see a disabled person who needed help.

The difference between this seizure and the ones in the movie theater or on the street is that people knew what to do then. When I convulse or collapse, people come running. They might not know much about seizures, but they know to cushion my head, and maybe call an ambulance.

Hospital TV shows love to have a seizure around the point the patient gets really sick—*House* in particular loved throwing this out three-quarters through an episode—so people recognize that convulsions mean someone is in trouble. When I have an absence seizure people don't connect me blankly staring like a rabbit in the headlights with a neurological disorder. This is where The Look comes in—being unequipped to recognize that what is happening to me is a medical issue, that I might be a vulnerable person in need of help.

I learned a saying recently from editor Dana: "you don't know until you know." As an eternal optimist, I like to think that people are generally good. The Look and inaction come from being unequipped; under-educated about the full swathe of disability experiences; or just not knowing how to help, worried about making things worse. That goes for how best to comfort a crying fluff ball as well as being able to recognize that my miscellaneous odd behaviors meant something serious was happening. It's ignorance, not malice. And so, I don't feel anger toward those people who didn't help. I just wish I could revisit them like a friendly Ghost of Christmas Past and tell them how I experienced that interaction, or lack thereof, so they could learn.

I grew up in a pretty atypical family. I wasn't diagnosed as autistic or with Hypermobile Ehlers-Danlos Syndrome (hEDS) until I was in my late twenties, but I showed all the hallmarks of both from a young age. My parents and sister are all invisibly disabled, the only hints of difference seen in a reaction to flashing lights, or the way they use a golf umbrella like a walking stick. My grandparents, aunts and uncles, and other miscellaneous relatives were also predominantly disabled people—that's a good batch of genetics for you.

Disability was, and is, the norm for me. My childhood memories are peppered with mundane, vaguely medical moments— helping stretch my dad's back to free his sciatic nerve, putting my sister in recovery position, and helping my mum reach things. Our bungalow wasn't a hospital by any stretch—it was a home, and these were all part of our day. Adjusting plans last minute, checking if someone needs help to do a task, learning the warning signs that they're struggling, accepting that today is just not a leave-the-house kind of day, and knowing that their pain can change in a moment are important ways to support disabled people, and are just part of my coming-of-age story. Admittedly, I think having this kind of relaxed-compassion to life made it much easier for me to cope with the changes to my body as I eventually became more disabled as an adult.

Invisible disabilities aren't so much invisible to me as quiet. I can catch them in the way someone stands with the weight on one hip, and know they're hypermobile—I like to say people with hEDS stand like a late-stage Jenga game. The way someone flaps their hands, wrings their clothes through their fingers, or taps out of a hug like my Nanna used to. The deep, bone-rattling sigh they make when they get onto the bus and see there are no seats.

On days when I'm out in London and feeling well, I look for these quiet signs. When I first moved to London, frustrated by the lack of support for people who need seats on the tube, I would eagle eye everyone boarding the train for a different kind of look—a weariness, a desperate burn in the eyes, the look that says "I need to ask for help, but I don't know how to." If I saw it and could stand, I'd jump out of my seat, asking if they would like it. The flash of relief and gratitude is one I've seen on my own face, reflected in the glassed darkness when someone does the same for me.

> **INVISIBLE DISABILITIES AREN'T SO MUCH INVISIBLE TO ME AS QUIET.**

I was just one of the many people involved in campaigning for a Please Offer Me a Seat badge for the London transportation network, arguing that it meant people didn't need to be fluent in other people's pain; they just needed to look for the badge. I also quietly hoped that people would start to associate the badge with that tired desperation, and would learn to see it on its own, building up their compassion for fellow passengers.

All this experience and trying doesn't make me perfect. I still miss things, but I keep my eyes open, listen, and learn. If in doubt, I offer help—the embarrassment of an affronted stranger is better than leaving someone struggling. I'm actively trying to unlearn judgments that have snuck in without me realizing, which often contradict what I actually think.

I do think that the normalization of disability in my upbringing, on top of my own experiences, has attuned me to others' quiet needs. Essentially, it's familiarity. It's a combination of preexisting knowledge and knowing to listen where I lack it. It's what the people wearing The Look were lacking.

So, what can you do to dismantle that instinctive judgment and grow your compassion if you didn't grow up surrounded by disabled people?

The very first thing you should do, as with any marginalization you don't share, is to accept that you probably know less about their experiences than you think you do. Not only do you not have firsthand experience of their life, but the media we consume—books, film, television, the news, and even charity communications—are usually filtered through an abled lens.

> YOU'RE NOT EXPECTED TO BECOME AN EXPERT AND THERE DEFINITELY WON'T BE A TEST, BUT IT'S GOOD TO UNDERSTAND WHAT PEOPLE AROUND YOU MIGHT BE GOING THROUGH, SO YOU CAN SUPPORT THEM.

Autism, for example, tends to be told by the carers, parents, siblings; this is why I edited *Stim*, an anthology of autistic people's writing—because everything I read was about us, not by us. This is replicated in many fields of disability, and means that historically our individual voices have been boosted less.

Second, start listening. This is potentially a huge project considering just how many disabilities there are, but think about the disabled people in your life, your school, your workplace, those you follow online. Listen to what they say about their experiences, and believe them. You're not expected to become an expert and there definitely won't be a test, but it's good to understand what people around you might be going through, so you can support them. There will be things that make no logical sense, but you are not their doctor nor in their body, so bite down that urge to question.

Our media constantly tells stories of people faking their disability, especially the news that reports every sensationalist story of benefits fraud—particularly where a claimed disability is involved—even though the rate of fraud, which is reported combined with error on their part, is usually less than 1%. In the UK, this has emboldened people to report on their neighbors who they suspect of fraud, which results in an immediate freeze in their money that can last weeks, even if there's no evidence of fraud.

Even I as a disabled person cannot explain why some days I can walk with limited pain, and others, like the day before I wrote this paragraph, it took me six hours to be able to sit upright. Ambulatory wheelchair users know this feeling particularly well, often being interrogated by perfect strangers about whether they are faking their disability.

I don't currently use a wheelchair day-to-day, but when I visited Disneyland Paris with my friends, getting up out of the wheelchair to walk to the bathroom definitely earned me a few of

The Looks from people who couldn't match up the two mes: the disabled wheelchair occupying me, and the walking me. Somewhat ironically, during the same trip but on a day when I wasn't using a wheelchair, a woman also in the disabled entrance to *Mickey's Christmas Big Band* remarked that they must be letting anyone in, implying that I wasn't disabled. Luckily my ferocious best friend leaped to my defense, and I hope that woman learned something from it. The people in the restroom couldn't match me visibly using a mobility aid but being ambulatory with being disabled, while the woman in the line couldn't equate disability with me standing without one. Sometimes it feels like you can't win! Living with a fluctuating disability is like living in a world of contradiction, and the best thing in my experience is for those around me to graciously adapt to my today.

It's worth saying that The Looks are not confined to train carriages and Disneyland Paris. One of the biggest problems disabled people face is disbelief from some medical professionals, which can leave us without care and support, which can make our disabilities worse and absolutely tanks our mental health. This is why it took me the best part of twenty-five years to get diagnosed as autistic, twenty years for Hypermobile Ehlers-Danlos syndrome, eighteen for endometriosis, ten years to recognize one type of my seizures were related to my blood pressure. Time and again I would ask doctors for help with chronic pain, periods that meant I blacked out, or the anxiety I felt having to get onto a commuter train, only for them to ignore what I was saying, instead tuning into their presumptions.

Many doctors have a habit of seeing a person with a list of problems as being a hypochondriac, as opposed to someone who might have a genetic predisposition that links them all together. I started pushing back against my misdiagnoses around the time I tried to access an autism diagnosis and was

sent to a child psychiatrist, despite being in my late twenties. I was fed up with hearing doctors tell me their preconceptions rather than anything that matched my experiences, but that's truly, truly exhausting. I was only able to do it because my partner had my back and because, to be frank with you, I'd decided enough was enough.

The thing you need to understand is that my experience isn't unique; most of my friends with invisible disabilities have similar stories, especially fat people who are always told to "just lose weight" no matter their condition.

Again, you are not expected to become an expert in all this, or launch the campaign for better disability training for medical staff (although if the fancy takes you, I certainly won't stop you); the thing you should do is empathize. Don't imply the doctor just didn't understand, or that perhaps we didn't phrase things right; this just adds to the medical trauma that many of us carry. Listen to, learn from, and support us.

The third point is, in my opinion, the one that requires the most work. It's about practicing catching your judgmental brain making an assumption, and interrogating it. And by this I don't just mean the obviously negative thoughts, but any thought you might have about what a particular disabled person might experience. Recognize it. Sit with it. Ask yourself where you learned this information. Was it from a disabled person, or from a movie, or something your parents said? How long ago did you hear it? Does it match up with what the people you have listened to say? Do you need to go learn more? This process can be uncomfortable, but it's important work, and core to being an ally to disabled people.

In practicing all these tools and expanding your compassion, you will be well on the way to both dismantling your judgment and being a great ally to disabled people.

11

"WHY DIDN'T ANYONE ELSE SAY ANYTHING?"

NAOMI AND NATALIE EVANS

"We have to repent in this generation not merely for the hateful words and actions of the bad people but for the appalling silence of the good people." — Dr. Martin Luther King, Jr., "Letter from Birmingham Jail," 1963

NATALIE

It was late October and I was at the train station in London traveling back to my small hometown by the sea. It was a sunny Friday afternoon, but the air was cold enough to see the condensation from my mouth when I breathed out.

I had just finished a full day of work that involved a lot of meetings, coffee, and dull conversation, so I was very tired and ready for the weekend ahead. I stood on the platform in my thick coat and a scarf, wishing I had driven that day. The clock turned 3:25, and two bright circle lights entered through the tunnel.

"Finally," I thought. I waited for passengers to get off before I stepped on the train and found two single seats available. Then I put in my headphones, tilted my head on the glass window next to me, and closed my eyes while the train sped off to the next stop.

As my podcast played I heard a faint announcement in the background as the train slowed down at the next stop. When I opened my eyes, I saw two white men, both wearing black coats, jeans, and carrying a supermarket bag which I imagine had the remaining cans of beer that they were holding in their hands. They were speaking like they were in a nightclub, where you have to shout over the music to hold a conversation. Other passengers noticeably shuffled their bodies and moved to attention. Ears pricked up—some people looked up and away quickly while others rolled their eyes to show their disapproval at the lack of train etiquette.

All I wanted was a quiet journey home. I hoped they wouldn't be on the train for much longer.

As I scanned the carriage once again, I noticed something that wasn't very unusual to me; everyone else was white. I am mixed-race. My dad is Black Jamaican and my mum is white British, so I have brown skin along with big curly afro hair. I grew up in a very white area in Kent where most of my life I was the only person—apart from my two sisters—that looked like me in the room.

The two men were two seats away from me. I could see them between the gap in the seats and the reflection of a man in a black jacket, still clutching his beer, in the train window. Once they sat down, I closed my eyes again, leaned back on the glass window, and tried to nap once more.

The nap didn't last very long. I was interrupted by the booming voice of the conductor asking for tickets. I took my headphones out and pulled out my train ticket, ready for when he approached. The train conductor was a Black man. It's not unusual for me to notice people's race; even though my town has become more diverse and multicultural, I am still surprised when I see a Black person in the area.

I smiled and passed over my train ticket, he gave me a nod and I nodded back. This is very normal in the Black community—it's like an acknowledgment, a code for "I see you, I understand, I get what it's like to be Black in this world." I watched him walk down the carriage, asking the other passengers for their tickets, and I looked at the two loud drunk men. In my gut I knew not to put my headphones back in.

You see, when you're used to being the minority in the room you tend to pick up on certain things when in public spaces. You know when situations feel unsafe or when people are hostile toward you. You sense when to not trust a person; it's an instinct and it's one that I've gotten very used to over the years.

The train conductor walked over to the two drunk men and said, "Tickets please." There was silence, so he repeated, "Tickets please," again silence. I stared at the man with the supermarket bag in between the train seats, snickering to his friend. The conductor repeated himself again, but this time his tone was agitated and short.

Finally, the man with the supermarket bag responded without looking up, "We are getting off at the next stop, mate."

The train conductor replied, "That's not how it works, it doesn't matter if you get off at the next stop, you still need the ticket before getting on the train."

This went back and forth for about 30 seconds. The conversation between them was getting much louder and at this point more people started to pay attention. My instincts were right. After the train conductor explained that they would need a ticket in order to continue the journey the man with the supermarket bag replied, "Did you get a f***ing passport to get into the country?".

It was at that point my ears pricked up like a cat when they hear it's time for a bath. I scrambled around in my pocket, got out my phone, and pressed record.

This was my second step of being an ally.

You see, step one was realizing that this was not a safe space for the conductor. Being an ally means anticipating when someone may need support. It's about understanding the power dynamics within a room.

The train conductor's face dropped; he had a combination of facial expressions—shocked, angry, and embarrassed. I could see in his face he didn't know what to do. The next five minutes were a blur; without the phone recording I don't think I would've been able to remember what happened next. As soon as I pressed record, the train conductor sat down next to the two drunk men.

I was very surprised when he decided to sit next to them. I wondered if it was to try and deescalate the situation, maybe coming down to their level meant that they could have a conversation, rather than standing over them intensifying an argument. He then asked in an upset and slightly angry voice, "What has me having a passport got to do with your train ticket?"

It was unclear what one of the men was trying to explain but it didn't matter by this point. What he had said was racist and he was not willing to apologize for it.

The train conductor's voice got louder and his hands became more expressive. He kept repeating, "What has me having a passport got to do with your train ticket?" He told the man that his comment was racist.

> BEING AN ALLY MEANS ANTICIPATING WHEN SOMEONE MAY NEED SUPPORT. IT'S ABOUT UNDERSTANDING THE POWER DYNAMICS WITHIN A ROOM.

The white man responded, "I've got two mixed-race children and this guy thinks I'm racist." The train conductor shook his head, gave a loud sigh, and stood up to walk away. He was finished; the man was not listening and now had brought out his get-out-of-jail-free card, his mixed-race children.

I can relate to this feeling in so many ways. Someone has said something offensive, you challenge it, but it's game over. Defensiveness kicks in. White fragility comes into play and there is nowhere to go but to walk away. Yet, the man with the supermarket bag was still not finished. "It's always the Black card with you innit."

My blood was boiling. I was raging and everything inside me wanted to explode. There were so many things about this situation that were problematic but to then bring in mixed-race children and the race card? I could not just sit there and record this incident anymore, I had to say something. Before I knew it I stood up and without a thought, I opened my mouth.

This was step three of my allyship that day. I didn't have a well-planned-out speech, but the fact that no one else spoke up meant whatever I said was better than silence.

"Are you listening to what you have just said, it's RACIST," I said in a loud voice. He sat there and looked at me with both hands on the table, one hand still clenched around his can of beer.

"Are you serious?" he replied.

> I COULD NOT JUST SIT THERE AND RECORD THIS INCIDENT ANYMORE, I HAD TO SAY SOMETHING.

I continued. "Just because you have mixed-race children does not give you the right to say what you just said. Why are you asking him if he had a passport? Would you have said that if he was white?"

The guy seemed to have an answer for everything: "But," "I," "Whatever," "I am not racist."

"What has your train ticket got to do with his passport?"

He looked away from me and hung his head, like a puppy who couldn't look at his owner after chewing up the sofa. He tried one more time, "Oh my god I can't say anything anymore . . ."

"Don't start playing the victim now. Explain why you said it."

He sat back and sighed. He had nothing, no answer that would get him out of this mess.

I think he was shocked that I challenged him. He got up and went to apologize to the train conductor. His friend stayed in his seat. He had not said one word throughout the whole incident. The man looked defeated; I think he knew he had messed up but it was too late, the damage was already done.

I sat down and I turned off the recording. I was shaking, my voice was shaking, my hands were shaking, my body was shaking, and I was utterly devastated.

These incidents were nothing new to me. I am used to them; however, the one thing that upset me the most, even more than having to challenge racist comments, was that not one other person intervened.

Not. One.

The woman sitting in front of me put a scarf around her head as if it would make her invisible. The man opposite me moved his newspaper closer to his face so that he could pretend he couldn't see what was happening. Two younger guys beside me looked shocked, like rabbits in the headlights, not knowing what to do or say.

When I looked around the carriage, people who were staring at me dodged my gaze. One woman looked at me in disgust and shook her head; clearly, I had ruined her journey home.

I decided to move carriages as I didn't want to be near any of them anymore. I sat down, still shaking, slammed my bag on the chair, and let out a big sigh. As the train slowed down to a stop, I looked out the window and saw the two men in their black jackets, still holding their cans of beer while walking away.

A few minutes later, the train conductor came over and thanked me, to which I responded, "There is nothing to thank me for. I am so sorry this happened to you." I explained I had it on video and if he needed, I could send it to him to report to the police. We then both carried on with the train ride, and it felt like the longest journey in the world.

When the train stopped at the next station and people got up to leave the carriage, a few people from the previous carriage walked over to me and said well done. I felt so angry. I wanted to respond with, "Where were you?," "Why didn't you say anything?," "This shouldn't be my fight."

Why were the only Black and Brown people (me and the train conductor) the ones to say something? Why didn't white people use their privilege in that moment?

As soon as I got off the train, I called my sister, Naomi. The person I knew would understand.

I told her the story and explained how embarrassed I was and that I thought I handled the situation terribly. I thought about all the things I could have said but it was too late.

However, Naomi asked the same question that I have asked many times growing up, when I left meetings at work, on nights out with friends, family gatherings, and even church socials. "Why did nobody else say anything?"

NAOMI

I was walking home from my local store when I answered the phone call from Natalie. I was expecting her to tell me what time she would be home, but instead I was met with a shaky voice and crying. Natalie is six years younger than me and I've always been a protective big sister. I stopped in my tracks and was instantly alert.

"What's wrong?" I quickly asked.

"Na, something horrible just happened on the train," she sobbed.

As I listened, I knew exactly what she was going to say. It wasn't unusual for me to hear about racist incidents. From ignorant phrases to outright violence, I have faced racism my whole life. It was something that I lamentably accepted as part of everyday life. It was something we as a family were used to and although it was still deeply upsetting, it was not surprising.

Every time a new incident happened it was another reminder of older ones, like opening up an old wound. The ignorant things people said to you at school that reminded you that you were the Brown girl. "You're colored/half-caste." "Can I touch your hair? It looks like cotton candy." "You're really well spoken." "Where are you really from?"

All of these incidents served to give the same reminder: you were not like them. You were "other" and as much as you tried to brush it off, your experiences would never be understood. I spent most of my teenage years trying to fit in but also knowing deep down that I wasn't really being myself.

My relationship with my hair was one of the most damaged. Constant straightening, chemicals, hair dye, and weaves, all in an attempt to look like the women I saw around me and in the magazines.

When I was growing up, hair, beauty, and fashion were centered around Eurocentric ideals, and there was scarcely any other representation and no Black hairdressers or salons. I would optimistically go to the white hairdressers clutching a photograph I had ripped out of a magazine, my mum tactfully trying to explain to me that my hair wouldn't go like that.

When I was about nine, a particular hairdresser who clearly had never touched afro hair before, ended up cutting most of it off. I was devastated. I remember seeing the hairdresser a few weeks later at the beach. She smiled and waved at my mum. Tears welled up inside of me. I was so angry with her. Did she not realize what she had done?

When I was growing up, other than my mum, there was never another white person who defended me. It was painful; it made me anxious, and at times I questioned my own sanity.

I went to a white majority school. It was also an all-girls school, which brought another dynamic—lots of teenagers trying to find their place in the hierarchy. Gossip, friendship break-ups, and navigating popularity, but race relations added another complication.

When I was eleven, a girl shoved past me to get to the paints in an art lesson. She was the kind of character who seemed to be able to do and say whatever she wanted with very little consequence. I shot her a dirty look and she turned to me and whispered, "You ni**er."

I was shocked and also had no idea what to do. If I told the other girls I couldn't be sure anyone would stick up for me. I looked over at Mrs. Peerless, our art teacher, who was probably in her sixties. She had a gray bowl cut, white overcoat, and glasses that sat at the end of her nose. She had a kind face. I decided she was my only hope. At least she would issue a detention or call the girl's parents.

TELLING SOMEONE WHO HAD JUST BEEN CALLED A RACIST INSULT THAT "WE ARE THE SAME" IS TO IGNORE THEIR VERY REAL EXPERIENCE AND DISMISS THEIR VALID EMOTIONS.

I took a deep breath and walked over to her. She ushered me into the corner of the studio and I explained what happened. Before I'd finished she shouted across the room and called the other student over. And as expected, she talked her way out of it. She said I misheard and she had called me a "piggler." The teacher looked at us both and loudly said for the class to hear, "We're all the same." That was the end of the matter. Well, it probably was for them.

Maybe the teacher thought she was doing the right thing at the time. I used to hear the "we're all the same" argument a lot. While we know race is a social construct, we also know that we are not all treated the same and we do not all have equal opportunities. Telling someone who had just been called a racist insult that "we are the same" is to ignore their very real experience and dismiss their valid emotions.

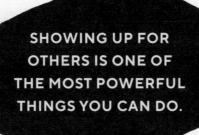

SHOWING UP FOR OTHERS IS ONE OF THE MOST POWERFUL THINGS YOU CAN DO.

At that moment my teacher should have been my ally. She should have taken the load off me and advocated on my behalf. At the very least, she should have spoken to that student about how violent that word is and checked in with me after the incident to see if I was okay. It's only on reflection, and now that I am a teacher myself, that I understand how badly she failed me.

Now, twenty-five years after this incident and many others, I understand it's not me with the problem. The lack of understanding about racism isn't my responsibility and I don't need to try and fit in with white people's expectations of me. The more we as BIPOC (Black, Indigenous, People of Color) or those who call ourselves allies challenge racism when we see and hear it, the less power it has. Showing up for others is one of the most powerful things you can do.

Allies would have supported the train conductor and Natalie that day. They would have stopped Natalie from being the only person to say something publicly. I wouldn't have needed to be the "shoulder to cry on," to relive the past trauma and painful memories we have endured throughout our life.

Allyship can show up in all different forms; however, in this case, we are talking about being a public ally. Racism needs to be challenged when it's seen or heard and not just by those who it's directed at. Silence is dangerous. It can imply you are complicit and in agreement with what is being said. So what makes people not do anything when they see racism?

A potential answer lies in the bystander effect or bystander apathy, a social psychological theory which states that the greater the number of people present in a situation, the less likely they are to intervene. It's also known as diffusion of responsibility. The more onlookers there are, the less personal accountability individuals will feel to take action. In short, everyone assumes someone else will speak out, so they don't have to. It would be a lie to say it's easy to speak up when someone is being racist.

It can be a daunting prospect, but one thing I have learned is that it only takes one person to make a difference.

NATALIE

Months had passed since the incident on the train. I had shown a few of my friends the video. Most of my friends are white and their responses are usually the same: "I can't believe it" and "I am so sorry." When I showed my Black friends, I warned them it was triggering. One of my friends told me I needed to put it online so he could share the video to his large Twitter following. I declined. I was still embarrassed by the way I handled things and I couldn't bear to see negative comments from online trolls.

A few weeks went by and the murder of Ahmaud Arbery happened in America. He was a Black man lynched by two white men while he was out running. They had taken it upon themselves to follow Ahmaud and shoot him dead in broad daylight in the street while an observer filmed the murder.

I was in my car waiting for my sister to come out of the supermarket when I first saw the video. I cried and cried, my stomach sick. As I looked online I saw the same comments I have heard my whole life: "I can't believe this is happening," "How does racism still exist?," and "So glad this doesn't happen in the UK." Some of these comments were coming from some of my closest friends and family. Did they really think this? Are people so naive that they believe racism doesn't exist here in the UK?

By the time I got home I had made up my mind. I told Naomi we needed to post the video of the train incident. I wanted people to see that racism was happening in the UK and to understand what we have to put up with nearly every day, whether it's directed at us or not. Naomi agreed. We both knew it was the right time.

I WANTED
PEOPLE TO
SEE THAT RACISM
WAS HAPPENING
IN THE UK AND TO
UNDERSTAND WHAT WE
HAVE TO PUT UP WITH
NEARLY EVERY DAY . . .

We discussed the consequences of people outside our circle seeing the video and the abusive things that might be said, but we were fed up with having the same conversations with each other. As I uploaded the video, my stomach felt queasy and my heart was thumping, like I felt when I was on the train. I clicked upload and from that moment our lives would change forever and in ways we would never have imagined.

Millions of people have now watched that incident. The video went viral, and as we watched it being shared all over social media Naomi looked at me and said, "We need to do more." The next day we started Everyday Racism, a safe space on social media for BIPOC in the UK to share their stories about everyday racist encounters.

When you have experienced a racist incident, one of the most difficult things is worrying about how people will respond when you speak up. You can be interrogated, accused of being too sensitive or overreacting—even if you are telling the truth.

To this day, there are many people who think racism is a thing of the past, and we want to make sure people can share their own accounts honestly and in their own words, so others don't feel alone. We now have followers from all over the world and we also share resources about how to be an effective ally in everyday life, as well as information to educate people on issues around racism.

You see, telling your story is a powerful way to be an ally and to help others become allies, too. You never know who it can impact and the lasting change it can have.

FROM AUTHOR, TO ALLY, TO CO-CONSPIRATOR

I.W. GREGORIO

I am a doctor, and for many years, I was an oppressor. Specifically, for years I unconsciously oppressed intersex folks—people born with biological conditions where their body doesn't conform to society's typical definition of male or female.

If you haven't heard of intersex before, you're not alone. My intersex friends like to say that the "I" in LGBTQIA has too long stood for invisible, and they're totally right. Too often, being intersex is confused with being transgender (the two can be related, but are not the same), or people assume that every intersex person has both a penis and a vagina (they don't).

> MY INTERSEX FRIENDS LIKE TO SAY THAT THE "I" IN LGBTQIA HAS TOO LONG STOOD FOR INVISIBLE, AND THEY'RE TOTALLY RIGHT.

I wrote my first young adult novel to bust intersex myths and increase intersex awareness. *None of the Above*, is about a sixteen-year-old girl who finds out right after she's voted Homecoming Queen that she was born intersex, and has XY chromosomes, internal testicles, and no uterus.

The basic take-home message of my story was that the girl next door could be intersex, and that one's chromosomes don't determine who one is, or who one loves. In the course of writing *None of the Above*, I spent countless hours on research and spoke with dozens of intersex people and parents.

If you had asked me when my book came out if I was an ally, I would have said, "Of course!" After all, I was a doctor trying to give voice to a patient whose story has rarely been told. I had donated to intersex support groups, provided their members with advance reader copies, and incorporated their feedback into the final draft.

But I could still do better at being an ally.

Looking back, I realize that the act of bearing witness to the struggles of a minority group—especially when one gets paid to do so—is not enough. When I began writing *None of the Above*, there were no other young adult books with intersex main characters. It was almost a decade before the #OwnVoices movement, but I should have given more thought to whether the story of an intersex teen was mine to tell. At the time, I justified pursuing the story because of my medical background, my personal experience, and an intense drive to make the concept of intersex accessible to young people.

BUT I COULD STILL DO BETTER AT BEING AN ALLY.

A decade later, there is finally a YA #OwnVoices intersex novel— Sol Santana's *Just Ash*, which is a mind-blowingly intense and insightful page-turner. And because it was written by an intersex person, it has a perspective and depth that my book could never have. If I could go back through time and insist that everyone who read *None of the Above* read *Just Ash*, I would.

Because if there's anything I've learned since publishing *None of the Above*, it's that part of being an ally is knowing when to center the experiences of intersex folks.

Intersex people have had doctors speaking for them for too long. Have you ever heard the term "paternalism?" It describes a relationship where a dominant person (for instance, a parent) makes the decisions for another person (for instance, a child).

I would argue that there is no more shameful evidence of how paternalistic the medical community can be than its treatment of intersex people, who for decades were lied to about their bodies and subject to medical procedures that were ill-advised at best, and unethical at worst.

I know intersex people who didn't find out about conditions they were born with until they were in their forties or fifties because doctors told their parents to conceal their diagnoses, since the truth of their "in-between" bodies would be too confusing. Others had their private parts operated on when they were babies, before they could give proper consent.

I didn't learn any of this in medical school. Instead, I was taught that being intersex was a disease to be fixed.

Rather than the word "intersex," which is preferred by many who identify that way, my medical textbooks used outdated and frankly insulting terms like "male pseudohermaphrodite" or "disorder of sex differentiation" to describe the different syndromes that fall under the intersex umbrella. I now understand that being taught to focus on intersexuality as being a disease or a hormone abnormality was the first step in dehumanizing intersex folks.

Instead of being exposed to the idea that the vast majority of intersex kids can become healthy adults without surgical intervention, I learned that their bodies were something that needed to be altered. Instead of being taught that intersex conditions were simply a natural variation in the fabric of humanity, my medical textbooks practically fetishized them as medical "zebras" (a term doctors sometime use for rare conditions that are not often encountered), focusing instead on the medications and operations that could make them more "normal."

Rather than learning that peer support, family counseling, and psychological care are the most critical elements of intersex care, and that most surgical treatment can be successfully delayed until the child is old enough to consent, I learned about potentially cancerous organs to remove and surgeries that could be performed on babies with congenital adrenal hyperplasia (CAH) to make their genitals conform to what a girl's clitoris and vagina "should" look like.

Here's irony: On the same campus where I pledged on my first day of medical school to "do no harm or injustice," I was taught that intersex bodies should be subject to surgeries—still currently performed at some medical centers in the US—that are now considered by the United Nations to be human rights violations.

In fact, the more intersex adults I meet, the more I realize that medical professionals have done the intersex community much more harm than good. You'd be hard pressed to meet an intersex person who doesn't shudder when thinking about going to see a doctor.

I knew none of this when I treated my first intersex patient; everything I knew about intersex could have filled maybe half a page of a notebook, and much of that information was misguided and inaccurate.

It wasn't until I took care of my first intersex patient—let's call her Orchid—that I realized how woefully my medical education had prepared me.

I met seventeen-year-old Orchid in a brief twenty-second interaction, just before she was rolled back into the operating room for a surgery to remove her gonads. I still remember the glee with which my attending doctor spoke about the case in morning rounds: "Ilene, this is a great teaching case. It's a patient with androgen insensitivity syndrome," or AIS.

I immediately recognized AIS as an often tested topic from my exam prep (and ultimately it was the condition I gave my main character in *None of the Above*): A child is born XY (with typically male chromosomes), but grows up looking like a girl (though, like boys, they don't have a uterus and have testicles instead of ovaries) because their cells can't identify and properly react to testosterone.

Historically, these testicles were thought to have a higher rate of cancer, and for decades CAIS* patients like Orchid had their testes removed in their teenage years, though recently these procedures have been shown to be mostly unnecessary.

I assisted Dr. X in doing the surgery, and then rushed around to do my laundry list of duties as a junior resident. Orchid didn't cross my mind again until a week later, when I saw her name on my list of patients to see in my post-op clinic.

I was at our county hospital, a public hospital where many patients are uninsured, and sometimes undocumented. It wasn't a surprise that Orchid's parents weren't in her room when I peeked in. I asked her how she was doing.

---

*CAIS stands for Complete Androgen Insensitivity Syndrome. People with CAIS usually have a typically female external appearance. In PAIS, or Partial Androgen Insensitivity Syndrome, sex characteristics can be less typical.

"Good," she said noncommittally. She didn't seem thrilled to be there. Not nervous, just bored.

"Can I look at your incisions?" I asked her. Her wounds—a pair of three-inch lines just below her bikini line in her groin—were healing well.

Two questions later, having exhausted the usual post-op checklist, I asked her, "Do you have anything else you want to ask me?"

She shook her head.

Red klaxons started going off in my mind. Wait, what? She was just diagnosed with an extremely rare condition, one that ensures that she will never have a biological child, and she doesn't have any questions?

It being the first time I'd exchanged even monosyllables with her, I had no idea what my attending surgeon had told her in her previous visit.

"Did Dr. X mention anything about having to take any hormone replacement?" I asked her, my voice shaking a little bit. I realized that if she said yes, I actually had no idea which hormone type and dose to give her.

She said no.

"Okay, well, let me go look over your chart and I'll see what he recommends."

I fled the room, heart pounding with my ignorance, and consulted with Dr. Google (Dr. X was actually not in the clinic that day, and honestly probably would not have had the answers I sought).

The Internet gods, and the pioneering intersex activists who used the power of the world wide web to form coalitions and create a collective voice that could not be ignored, saved me. A UK-based group called the Androgen Insensitivity Syndrome Support Group had created a handout on AIS basics, as well as information on how to connect to peer support.

I've said it probably a hundred times in presentations and book talks: The best thing I did that day was give Orchid that support group handout.

I did, of course, consult the medical literature to see what hormones to recommend (turns out, there are no well-studied regimens for women with CAIS, and people resort to using the same meds given to women who have gone through menopause). I explained that because she didn't have a womb, that she would not be able to have biological children, but she could still have a family through adoption if she wanted to.

Orchid barely seemed to register the information I presented. I couldn't tell if it was because she had heard everything I'd said before, or if she just wanted to be done already.

"Do you want me to talk to your parents?" I asked her.

"Nah," she said, shrugging.

"Well, please do reach out to the support group. You're not alone." I tried to set her up for a follow-up with a primary doctor and an endocrinologist.

A minute later she was gone. I never saw Orchid again, but I've thought about her countless times since.

Over the next few months, I went back to the AIS support group website and started reading through some of the personal essays posted by group members. There were harrowing stories of people whose parents concealed their diagnoses and lied to them about the surgeries they had as children. One woman discovered she was intersex through a sexual assault, others turned to substance abuse to deal with the stress of learning their diagnosis.

In anecdote after anecdote, people talked about how lonely and isolated they felt, how freakish, until they were able to connect with other intersex people.

I'VE REALIZED THAT SPREADING AWARENESS IS ONLY A SMALL PART OF WHAT AN ALLY CAN DO.

Around the same time, the South African runner Caster Semenya was outed by the press as being potentially intersex, and I was appalled by the way the media sensationalized the story, and stigmatized her intersex body. I started asking myself what would happen if my own child (I was pregnant at the time) was born intersex, and above all, continually wondered what became of Orchid. Did she have a boyfriend or girlfriend? What did she tell them?

Wanting to shed light on the topic in a compassionate way that would appeal to teens (who are by and large much more accepting of sexual and gender fluidity than their parents), I started writing the novel that would turn into *None of the Above*.

I'll go to my grave incredibly proud that my novel introduced the concept of being intersex to tens of thousands of people, but over the years I've realized that spreading awareness is only a small part of what an ally can do. Especially with Sol Santana's *Just Ash* coming out, I'm less inclined to promote my own book, and I am becoming more aware of my place within the intersex movement.

Right now, that means amplifying the voices of my intersex friends, and using the small amount of clout I have as a doctor to make sure that my medical colleagues hear loud and clear what their patients have to say to them. Make no mistake—fighting for the underdog is hard, exhausting work. Burnout is ridiculously high among activists, and my role as ally is to give my energy and raise my voice when I can.

The publication of my novel gave me the credentials to be able to speak at universities like Yale, Stanford, University of Michigan, and UC Davis, and in each of those institutions I made certain to

"IF WE AREN'T ALLIES, WHO WILL BE?"

both highlight the injustices that medicine has perpetrated on the intersex community, and also to share the stage with an intersex person to talk about their experiences and expose the doctors of the future to the knowledge that I never had.

At one of my early presentations, I met with polite skepticism from a pediatric urologist who was shocked that my intersex friend had never had her gonads removed. "You've never needed replacement hormones?" he asked, clearly dubious.

"Nope," said Emily, smiling her dazzling smile.

It seemed like what I was doing was helping. I could feel a shift in the way my medical colleagues talked about intersex conditions as public awareness grew through the efforts of interACT: Advocates for Intersex Youth, which worked with Buzzfeed to create a viral "What is Intersex" video that generated millions of hits. And consulted on MTV's *Faking It*, which had the first recurring intersex character on television.

With two intersex women and one mother of an intersex child, I gave one of the most impactful presentations of my life at the Society of Pediatric Urology—revealing the gaps in medical education and intersex care, and asking my fellow urologists, "If we aren't allies, who will be?"

At that meeting, I watched presentations from hospitals where my peers still perform surgeries to reduce the clitoris size of intersex babies. These procedures are irreversible, and have historically been plagued by high complication rates, including the side effects of chronic pain, discomfort during intercourse, and inability to orgasm.**

A few years later, I was invited to be a board member of interACT, and began to more intentionally raise money to fund their astounding policy advances and media awareness raising.

The game changer in the intersex rights movement was a landmark Human Rights Watch report that explicitly called for the US "to end . . . all surgical procedures that seek to alter the gonads, genitals, or internal sex organs of children with atypical sex characteristics too young to participate in the decision, when those procedures both carry a meaningful risk of harm and can be safely deferred."

That's when I started to learn what it meant to move beyond allyship—and started becoming a co-conspirator. Being a co-

---

**Some proponents of surgery argue that techniques have improved with so-called "nerve sparing" procedures, but as of yet there are no long-term studies to show that these children have been truly spared the poor outcomes of intersex children in the past.

conspirator means moving from listening and supporting my intersex friends to actively fighting on their behalf.

For me, it means not being afraid to ask for meetings with the President and President-Elect of the Society of Pediatric Urology, where they attempt to shame you in front of your program director by suggesting that your decision to advocate for the delay of surgery is a) naive and b) not medically sound. (To be clear, there is no good scientific data to support early surgery on intersex children. No randomized controlled trials of outcomes, only biased case series or retrospective surveys of parental attitudes.)

Being a real co-conspirator means not being ashamed of crying in front of said colleagues, and trying to broker some sort of detente between them and your activist friends.

Being a real co-conspirator means only minding a little bit when you realize you have to take a public position on an intersex person's right to bodily autonomy, and call out your colleagues' intellectual dishonesty in front of the California State Senate while it argues a bill to protect intersex children from unnecessary surgeries.

Being a real co-conspirator means that when the people who educated you frame the battle for intersex human rights as an "Us" vs. "Them" fight, you choose to stand with Them.

"They" are interACT: Advocates for Intersex Youth, which has been explicitly labeled as a "radical LGBT" group by doctors, but which is viewed by many, including myself, as a force for good in the universe.

I'm one of them now, and I agree that we are radical! We subscribe to the radical view that intersex bodies are to be celebrated rather than swathed in secrecy and shame.

I have been told that our push to delay surgery is "anti-choice."

We find this laughable, and an infuriating co-opt of the language of *Roe v. Wade*. In fact, interACT believes in the child's right to choose what their parts are, and that parents should not be able to dictate what their children's genitalia look like when there is a reasonable chance that their gender preferences may be fluid.

This is how I know that I've finally become a co-conspirator: Because by fighting for what I believe in, I've pissed off many of my doctor friends and colleagues, possibly to the point of damaging my professional reputation. So now, when I use the word "we," I don't mean the medical community that I've worked in for almost twenty years; I mean the rock star community of intersex activists, whose bravery and resilience are holding my profession accountable for its past sins.

13

LUPE

AIDA SALAZAR

I grew up watching impromptu drag shows in my living room. The shows transformed the humble living room of my childhood into a grand ballroom where glamor and performance reigned. My mother, a very Catholic, very straight, and cis gender traditional Mexican woman surrounded herself, surprisingly, with many male friends. They all happened to be gay. Her closest friend was Lupe; he was like family. He and Mami knew one another from the time they were children and lived in the same pueblo in Mexico. They played with the rag dolls Mami's oldest sister would make for them. They each immigrated to the United States for different reasons, yet they found one another in Los Angeles and picked up right where they left off.

I never questioned what it was that made Mami and Lupe's relationship so unconditionally sweet until recently. What made up their alliance? They couldn't have been more different. Mami lived such a traditional role as the stay-at-home mother of seven children and the wife of her childhood sweetheart. She was pious and was so devoted to her household duties and family that she often went without any number of comforts or conveniences so that we could have what we needed.

Lupe lived a different life than Mami. He was unabashedly out as gay, effeminate, independent, and unafraid. He had been disowned by his own family in Mexico. They beat him and even

LUPE CAME TO THE UNITED STATES TO FLEE FROM THAT HATE AND HE DEVELOPED A BIG AND BEAUTIFULLY DIVERSE COMMUNITY OF GAY MEXICAN MEN IN 1970S AND 1980S LOS ANGELES. AND THEN THERE WAS MY MOTHER AND ALL OF US.

sent him to jail (a thing you could do to your children in Mexico in the 1960s) simply for being gay. Lupe came to the United States to flee from that hate and he developed a big and beautifully diverse community of gay Mexican men in 1970s and 1980s Los Angeles. And then there was my mother and all of us.

Mami never treated him differently because of who he loved. His gayness did not faze her, in fact, she welcomed him as he was and was privy to details of his personal life. Lupe often told my mother he had been certain of his sexuality since he could remember and that he never wished being gay on anyone. The humiliation he suffered as a child and young man during the 1960s wounded him deeply. Mami empathized with him, because she knew what it was to feel ashamed about something you cannot control.

While entirely different, Mami's experience of shame came when her mother (my grandmother) had multiple extramarital affairs. Mami's young life was stained with an unspoken scarlet letter. She was mistreated in the pueblo—it was assumed she was a promiscuous girl because of her mother's behavior. Ironically, it was my grandmother's need to express her sexuality as a free woman that made her transgression so painful to Mami. Yet and still, this understanding of inculpable shame bound Lupe and Mami together to the point where Mami was willing to ignore tradition and religion for the sake of friendship and compassion. There was also something else at play, the things that make up a family—their shared acts of kindness to one another, unconditional support through hard times, and their shared experiences of joy.

Whenever Mami would deliver a baby, and she had four in the US, Lupe would come to provide help by cooking for us, by tidying up the house or sending us outside to play so Mami could rest. Lupe was a hair stylist and he'd cut our hair in wild '80s styles. He sold clothes out of the trunk of his car or his living room, and if we helped him he'd pay us with our choice of clothes or minimum wage. We felt loved and protected by him, though he would not hesitate to scold us if we were ever out of line.

> **THERE WAS ALSO SOMETHING ELSE AT PLAY, THE THINGS THAT MAKE UP A FAMILY—THEIR SHARED ACTS OF KINDNESS TO ONE ANOTHER, UNCONDITIONAL SUPPORT THROUGH HARD TIMES, AND THEIR SHARED EXPERIENCES OF JOY.**

By the same token, Lupe relied on Mami for warm, home-cooked meals, for the feeling of family, children, and closeness that he didn't have any longer. Papi understood how close Mami and Lupe were and never questioned his presence in our lives. Lupe was family. That's why it was not uncommon for Mami to have Lupe and his friends over for dinner, for singing along to music that blared from the old cassette player, and telling lively stories about their adventures. Lupe and his friends brought so much joy into our home—and laughter, endless amounts of laughter.

The drag shows were electrifying performances. Lupe and his friends—Chuyina, Petronila, Bruno—had an instant audience with Mami, her seven children, and sometimes Papi, when he wasn't working the night shift. They would emerge from Mami's bedroom dressed in her clothes and makeup, singing and dancing, and lighting up the room.

They lip-synced to Mexican pop songs and American ones as well, though most of the men hardly spoke English. Through the wonder of drag, they melted down any notion of rigidity around gender. I sat there, happily among my siblings, cheering and paying witness to their brilliance, their magic, their freedom. Those were among the most grace-filled moments of my childhood.

At about six or seven years old, though I was a girl, I wanted to be like my only brother. I wanted to wear my hair short like him. I wanted to wear jerseys like him. I wanted to play football like him and be like just one of the guys. Traditional Mami did not bat an eye. She let me be who I wanted to be. She never questioned my clothes and was relieved not to have to comb another one of her daughters' long hair. Lupe concurred and helped keep my hair short and feathered as was the style in the late '70s. I wanted to be comfortable and look tough. At home, no one cared about my gender expression.

The problems came from my extended family, and mostly from friends at school who mocked me for being a "tomboy" or "marimacha," which is Spanish for "dyke." I remember feeling hurt by their words because they seemed derogatory, though I honestly didn't understand what they meant. I understood the negative energy they gave off. It puzzled me that the same kids who went to school with me and were part of the same Catholic community who said to "do unto others as you would have them do unto you" could be so mean for no reason.

Then, when I first kissed a girl in the fifth grade, I was further sent into a cloud of confusion. Beatriz was a sweet girl who made me spin with happiness, and I know she felt the same by the way she looked at me, or how she nuzzled my nose when we would chase each other and tumble into one another when we fell. Our kiss felt natural, exciting, and sweet for that moment. But Beatriz burst into tears right after kissing me behind the school bungalows. She said she was going to burn in hell because of our kiss. I started crying, too, because I believed her. Every Catholic bone in my body was certain of it. I allowed her to pull me into the girl's bathroom so we could wash our mouths out with soap. Rinsing my mouth out seemed to scrub away my desire to express my true self. It was right after that fifth-grade girl kiss that I subconsciously gave in to the expectations of school friends and family. I began to grow my hair longer and wear dresses again. I buried my feelings of bisexuality and my boyish gender expression down deep.

During that time, I was awakened in the middle of the night to a commotion in the living room. Lupe and his friends had been in a fight while out at a party not too far from our house. Their stylish clothes were covered in blood and their faces were swollen in some places. Mami was hurriedly dressing their wounds.

I only peeked in from the hallway, but when they saw me, Lupe rushed over, gently placed one arm around my shoulders and consoled me. "I'm fine. Nada pasa. Don't be scared." He joked, "You should see the other guys! They forget that we are men and can defend ourselves, too."

I laughed along with them at the time, but that moment filled me with a growing understanding. It reaffirmed that the freedom that inspired me to kiss Beatriz, and which I experienced in my home by witnessing drag shows, was not as accepted everywhere. But furthermore, the world was actually cruel to folks whose genders or gender expressions were fluid or who

OUR KISS FELT NATURAL, EXCITING, AND SWEET FOR THAT MOMENT. BUT BEATRIZ BURST INTO TEARS RIGHT AFTER KISSING ME BEHIND THE SCHOOL BUNGALOWS. SHE SAID SHE WAS GOING TO BURN IN HELL BECAUSE OF OUR KISS. I STARTED CRYING, TOO, BECAUSE I BELIEVED HER.

were queer in any way, and some of our scariest opponents were Catholics and Christians in our own Latinx community.

Later, when I was a teenager, Lupe was diagnosed with HIV— a deadly virus devastating the gay community. Not much was known about the virus at the time. Because it was afflicting a disproportionate number of gay men, many stigmas and prejudices emerged from not only the Latinx community but also from the world at large.

The puritanical messages that already condemned homosexuality or queerness exploded with absolute cruelty. Those who had previously been tolerant of gay men were now shunning them and shaming them out of an unfounded fear that they, too, would contract the virus.

Lupe's mother, after a long estrangement, had made amends with him, but then she once again turned her back on him when he was diagnosed. Lupe's mother believed it was God's wrath that made him sick as punishment for being gay.

Lupe's circle of friends began to perish from the disease, too, but there was one person who never left his side: Mami. She faithfully did practical things like driving him to his many medical appointments or to the pharmacy. She made sure he was well nourished and often sent us to his apartment, only a couple blocks away, with warm stews.

When his disease took hold and he could no longer care for himself, she gave him sponge baths, changed his bedsheets and bedpan, and spoon-fed him. Perhaps most importantly, however, she remained his confidant, his dearest friend. She sought to bring laughter into his life no matter how sick he became. What's more, Mami defended Lupe against anyone who dared speak poorly of him.

THERE ARE DEEP WOUNDS
THAT OUR OWN COMMUNITIES
INFLICT UPON US WHEN WE DON'T
OPERATE FROM A PLACE OF LOVE,
UNDERSTANDING, OPENNESS, AND
ALLYSHIP. I CARRY THE LESSONS THAT
MAMI AND LUPE'S FRIENDSHIP TAUGHT
ME INTO MY LIFE AS AN ADULT, FRIEND,
MOTHER, WIFE, AUTHOR,
AND ARTS ACTIVIST.

Once, Mami got into an argument with Lupe's older brother when Mami called to ask him to go and see Lupe, because Lupe did not have much time left to live. His brother, a staunch, macho Catholic, refused. I remember Mami begging him to draw on his compassion and on the bonds of family. When he continued to refuse, she became angry and told him off. She ended by saying, "May God forgive you for abandoning your own brother. At least he will always have me." Mami never broke her promise.

Mami and Lupe's friendship left an indelible imprint on my life. Her commitment to her dear friend, her almost brother, is among the greatest examples of allyship I've ever known. There are deep wounds that our own communities inflict upon us when we don't operate from a place of love, understanding, openness, and allyship. I carry the lessons that Mami and Lupe's friendship taught me into my life as an adult, friend, mother, wife, author, and arts activist. I pass them on in my work, as a tribute to little tomboy me who felt dirty for kissing a girl, for Lupe who felt my mother's allyship when others turned their back on him, for those who don't know how to fight against a society that wants to harm or demean them for who they truly are.

My life and this essay are dedicated to help others feel what I once felt as a child, watching a drag show dismantle rigid notions of identity and being filled with the grace of freedom.

"DID YOU KNOW GANDHI WAS RACIST?"

SHARAN DHALIWAL

I was sitting in a local coffee shop, waiting for a friend. She was running late. She was always running late. I looked in my bag for a book, a notepad—anything to distract myself with, knowing full well I was only carrying a bottle of water and packet of tissues.

"Sharan!!"

She had arrived; standing over me, with open arms, expecting an embrace. I did, of course; hugs are one of my favorite things to share with others.

"Did you know Gandhi was racist??"

My butt had barely landed back on my seat before my white friend made the declaration. I stared at her, but I didn't respond at first. I wasn't sure what to say. Not because I was ashamed, but because I was horrified that she assumed I didn't know. Like she had discovered a secret about my community that I was oblivious to. I was appalled that my activism was so limited, that white people around me didn't know about my concern over the idolization of Gandhi despite his racist comments.

I had already started working on my magazine *Burnt Roti*: a South Asian opinion and art publication, to help get underrepresented voices into the mainstream. It was a chance for people to speak about their identities, formed from their history and ancestors. I was doing talks, writing articles, and laying down the foundation of safety for many South Asians to feel comfortable enough to have these discussions. Before this, the only real representation in magazines was for Bollywood or your apparent inevitable wedding. There were obviously places for people to feel recognized; I'm not saying *Burnt Roti* was "the first ever" or "the only" platform for South Asian people, but it helped create a space for people to find each other.

I was used to having uncomfortable conversations that came from my magazine, such as: "why only South Asians? What if I want to write about when I went to India and saw some messed up stuff?" or "you can't hold your party at this venue all of a sudden now that we realized what your magazine is about." I'm used to talking about colorism, racism, identity issues, lacking empathy to other generations and their struggles, having a questionable attitude to immigration, and so on. I was used to all this and yet . . . this got to me.

"Yeah," I muttered back at her. I had to ready myself for the rest of the conversation. I could feel a phantom eye roll permanently plastered on my face, but I remained stoic.

She smiled and took a deep breath as I drew out a sigh.

"I read this morning that he had some pretty racist beliefs about Black people . . ."

She was on a roll. I turned the volume down on her and my mind wandered to the folders in my brain that had filed those pieces about Gandhi's comments on how he considered Black people as inferior. I wonder if she knew about the folder that sat in my brain about his sexual activities. She can do her own research on that; it seemed to give her an energy I've never seen in her before.

"Did you know?" She had finished and was looking directly in my eyes as I sipped my hot chocolate. I raised a finger as I finished gulping down the still-too-hot hot chocolate, burning my tongue. I smiled at her.

"Yeah, of course." I was still smiling. Why did I have to smile so much?

"I've never heard you talk about it!"

My smile disappeared.

I was stuck between two problems here. The first was that I didn't want to have to sit down with every white friend I had to discuss racism within my community. While work had to be done to unlearn and relearn histories and ideologies taught to our own community, I didn't want to do the work for white people. I was adamant that they should know better and teach themselves, instead of lazily hoping people of color will lay their trauma out on the figurative table.

But I had a literal table here between us and I wondered if my silence on Gandhi was my consent to anti-Blackness. It is an issue in South Asian history and in modern day—where many of us have anti-Black attitudes. Instead of crying "discrimination" from white people, should I be talking to her about Gandhi?

Sure, I've spoken about it before and I've had these conversations, but I felt energy drain from me. There's no real difference from my work and personal life—I find they both coexist naturally without any force, but gotta say . . . I wished she was paying me for this. I had bought my own hot chocolate. Maybe I should invoice her? More than anything, I wanted to catch up with her about her ex. I wanted gossip and laughter and relief from my everyday, but here I was yet again, cornered into my activism. Am I always an activist, even when I'm seeking moments of joy?

Is asking that further complicity? Am I the only Indian person she knew to ask about this? Did that matter? My mind ran through millions of questions as I stared back at her.

> **LIFE IS HARD. WHAT I LEARNED IS THERE'S ALWAYS SPACE TO LOOK AT HARDSHIPS BEYOND MY OWN.**

I was scared that I looked scared. I wasn't scared of talking about Gandhi's early racist views and comments he had made—when I had spoken about it in front of white people, she didn't happen to be there. Thinking about it, she had never attended any of my events. I pulled up a list in my head of all my white friends, and wondered how many were informed about Gandhi and how many I had to approach about it.

It upset me that a white person had instigated so much emotion in me about my activism, but if you don't regularly examine the work you do and criticize yourself, someone else will.

As a younger person, still coming to terms with her identity (I came out as bisexual in my thirties) and not having a handle on my mental health (I could list it all here, but that's another essay), I found myself to be mute on many political and social topics.

"Life is so hard!" I would exclaim regularly. Life was hard. Life is hard. What I learned is there's always space to look at hardships beyond my own. I was very self-involved in my pain, refusing to share it with others; like a trophy I never asked for.

While sitting in that quaint coffee shop with my friend, I was transported back to when I was in my early teens, listening to a conversation between guests and my family. An aunt and uncle who I had never seen before, but assumed were dear friends because they were eating my samosas, sat in the living room. The aunty was over-dressed for a simple visit, her jewels glistened at us as we looked down at our T-shirts and visibly rolled our eyes. The inexplicable power to accept eye rolls as a compliment are embedded in every aunty. It may seem harsh to roll our eyes so visibly, but it wasn't just for our benefit, but for her to know she made enough of an impact. The uncle sat neutrally next to her, speaking only to confirm everything she said.

As I passed around tea I stopped occupying my mind with what brand of lipstick the aunty was possibly wearing to hear her complain. She was explaining why she was slightly late, although no one cared; in reality, no one actually wanted guests, it's just something we had to do. She had seen moving vans outside her house and was investigating who her new neighbors were.

SOMETHING SANK INSIDE OF ME—I KNEW IT WAS DEEPLY WRONG FOR HER TO SAY THAT, BUT I ALSO KNEW I SHOULDN'T HAVE BEEN SILENT.

"I don't want Blacks living next door, all they do is drugs."

Something sank inside of me—I knew it was deeply wrong for her to say that, but I also knew I shouldn't have been silent. But I was. My privilege allowed me to. If I said anything, I would have been told to keep quiet—to be subservient, because not only are women, especially younger women, forbidden the luxury of opinions, they are especially not allowed when it goes against the norm. The norm here is anti-Black racism.

Let's not get it twisted; I wasn't in any way an outspoken activist at that age, nor had I unlearned many behaviors that were forced on me. I don't look back and think, "why didn't I speak up?" I knew I would never have then. It took me a long time to get to a stage of taking the lens and pointing it inward. After spending a lifetime noticing and being outraged by racism, sexism, and homophobia, it wasn't until I got older that I looked at my own activities.

I came up with a drug-related comeback recently—the drug pandemic is so prevalent in Punjab (where my family is from), they made a Bollywood film about it (*Udta Punjab*).

"Black people do drugs? Doesn't Punjab have one of the worst drug problems in the whole of India?"

Thirty-six-year-old me smiles smugly. Fifteen-year-old me is busy crying over that one sad Blink 182 song.

Lots of heads nod in response and a quiet agreement is acknowledged between everyone there. I go straight to my room and think about the comment. "I don't want Blacks living next door" kept playing over and over in my head. They weren't afforded the liberty of being considered people, they were "Blacks." It must have been easier for them to enact such violent racism when they dehumanize Black people.

It's never brought up again. I don't mention it to my family and they don't to me. It was a comment that passed through the lips of someone who had immigrated to a country that had created such a hostile environment that fear sat heavy in their hearts. Alongside the fear is a long history of anti-Black racism that predates the rule of the British Raj.

But before the colonial rule of the British Raj, a lot of South Asia had a problematic relationship with skin color. The biggest-selling beauty product in India is a skin lightening cream, which is marketed to South Asians who are darker skinned. Promoted by Bollywood stars and influencers, its message is clear—if your skin is dark, you should lighten it. It tells you to attain a beauty standard that wasn't built for us. In 2020, the parent company sent out a press release stating that they are changing the name of the brand in a misguided attempt to remain relevant in the wake of the global protests against racism, sparked by George Floyd's death. They know very well that changing the name does nothing, the stamp has been made and the rhetoric hasn't changed—Indians should be striving to whiteness. So, this discrimination is deep within us and these issues need to be examined, torn apart, and thrown away. I spent a lot of my childhood striving to whiteness by rejecting my culture, refusing to celebrate it or speak about it. The n-word noticeably became a customary word used by persons in my life, and though I rejected this acceptance, unable to utter it from my own lips, I allowed it to pass through others. I would make jokes discriminating against my own people, including immigrants, as if I were better than them. I now wonder about the culture I was rejecting. Maybe I wasn't rejecting my culture after all, but was rejecting these anti-Black attitudes instead. Although anti-Blackness lived deep in our history, it seemed as if it was coming to the surface in such a violent way.

Don't get me wrong, I love to blame everything on colonialism—in addition to it being deeply satisfying, it also rings true with the injustices that are faced today. Colonialism isn't just a historical act, it's being practiced now. We are governed, from our land to our bodies and our minds; whether we're told to look a certain way or we aren't afforded basic human rights, we are not free people.

In my thirties I created my magazine *Burnt Roti*—to allow people from my heritage to discuss stigmatized topics such as mental health, sexuality, and identity. The magazine was created in a moment of boredom. I had left my job, started an animation agency that was criminally underpaid for every project I managed to get, and was becoming increasingly aware of the different expectations for women of color in the creative industry, which happened to be dominated by cis white men (surprise, surprise). Crucially, that was the exact time I was interviewed about the nose job I had ten years prior, and the concept of ethnic cleansing through plastic surgery, for *Cosmopolitan* magazine.

That was the moment things changed for me. I started to confront a lot of dilemmas I saw within myself, which related to gender, sexuality, and race. I began a journey of understanding more about my position within the world, as a British Indian woman. I saw the inconsistencies of privilege and opportunities, which have always existed, but that I had previously kept my eyes closed to.

> I SAW THE INCONSISTENCIES OF PRIVILEGE AND OPPORTUNITIES, WHICH HAVE ALWAYS EXISTED, BUT THAT I HAD PREVIOUSLY KEPT MY EYES CLOSED TO.

So *Burnt Roti* was created to allow myself to understand and learn more about these inconsistencies, as well as give a platform for South Asians to be seen. We began working primarily in the creative world—talking to writers, actors, painters, illustrators, and so on. It then became a global think piece on South Asian culture, be it about queer identity or anti-Blackness. I didn't expect it, but the trajectory of *Burnt Roti*'s global success was very quick and I was contacted by a lot of people who thanked me for creating this publication, and more who simply wanted to talk to me more about the idea behind it. It had inspired many people to have conversations, build organizations, and create art themselves.

Very quickly I saw a lot of essays submitted that related to navigating a British and South Asian identity and it made me wonder about my own. I would think back to my teens and consider what elements of Indian culture I had embraced and whether I truly understood my heritage.

The biggest hurdle I found when questioning my own identity was my complicity to anti-Blackness. In 2020, we released issue three labeled in bold "Anti-Blackness in South Asian communities" with the words "anti-Blackness" in large font on the cover. When I first started talking about this issue, I was faced with comments from other South Asians. They would ask whether I was throwing my community under the bus. I would reply that we are already under a bus, I'm just trying to pull us out.

> THEY WOULD ASK WHETHER I WAS THROWING MY COMMUNITY UNDER THE BUS. I WOULD REPLY THAT WE ARE ALREADY UNDER A BUS, I'M JUST TRYING TO PULL US OUT.

> **WE NEED TO ACT, BUT OUR ACTIONS AREN'T TO SPEAK OVER THE MARGINALIZED—THEY ARE TO GIVE THE MARGINALIZED THE MICROPHONE.**

There was a deep fear in speaking about our own racism. Some people were concerned that it would allow others to continue to discriminate against us for not only our culture but also for our own racism. Others had buried the shame so deep inside of them it was painful to pull it out and face it. A couple of people told me that it would be a flop—no one would buy that issue. I didn't believe them. And I was right not to, because not only have I sold more of these copies in the first month of its release than any of our other issues, but it's been bought globally by people of all ethnicities. And crucially, by a lot of South Asians who are ready to learn and understand more about being an ally.

It was important that I didn't center myself or other South Asians in *Burnt Roti*'s anti-Blackness issue—although some of the articles were written by South Asians, the focus was on the Black community. We had mixed-race and Black writers talk about their experiences, marking moments of discomfort in their lives.

As an ally, and a light-skinned Indian woman, I know I need to take a backseat and allow the voices of others to come through. But I don't sit back comfortably, watching everything happen around me. This isn't the "this is fine" meme, this is real life and REAL LIVES. We need to act, but our actions aren't to speak over the marginalized—they are to give the marginalized the microphone. So, while these conversations are about the South Asian community, it's not about our struggles—it's about how we exacerbate the struggles of Black people. Instead of getting defensive we should listen, and with the insight we gain, turn our silence into action.

I look at my friend while I sip my hot chocolate, which has now cooled down significantly during the unbearably long, uncomfortable silence. I take a deep breath and I respond.

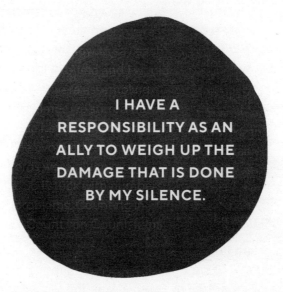

I HAVE A RESPONSIBILITY AS AN ALLY TO WEIGH UP THE DAMAGE THAT IS DONE BY MY SILENCE.

"Yeah, I've talked about it a few times, not sure you were there when I did. I actually tried speaking to my family about it but they didn't want to listen. It's really interesting because there's very little written about this; it seems we're selective about how we frame our idols."

I take another deep breath before I continue. Even though I was feeling emotionally distraught for having to have this conversation, it needed to be had. The government and state isn't explicitly harming my existence like it does to Black folk, so there is less pain in my words. I didn't want to have the conversation with a white person, but every person who I don't have the conversation with may open wounds for those who suffer more than me.

It's fun to say "Google is free," but people may just pass on those exact disposable words, instead of the knowledge of entrenched social and racial injustice in our society. I have a responsibility as an ally to weigh up the damage that is done by my silence.

15

LIFTING AS SHE CLIMBS

ANDREA L. ROGERS

I have wanted to be a published writer since the second grade. Whether it was creating and entertaining my friends with fan fiction about Def Leppard or writing songs and stories based on the music of Duran Duran, creating stories felt like the only work that mattered. Early in my writing journey the importance of having an ally never occurred to me.

I'm a citizen of the Cherokee Nation and for years I, personally, knew no other Native writers and had no allies in my journey. However, allies are as important in publishing as they are in making a more just world. And sometimes there are allies who work for justice by helping others tell their stories.

In 2012, books and media with Native content existed, but for the most part, the material was filled with stereotypes and inaccurately represented tribes and nations. This lack of representation meant Native students had fewer positive role models for their potential in the world, fewer places to imagine themselves, and few stories that honestly and accurately mirror their culture. As a way to help urban Native students stay or become connected with their culture, our school district's American Indian Education program hosted an "American Indian Camp" each summer. I taught Cherokee basket weaving and Indigenous literature to thirty urban Native kids from a variety of tribes. Two of my older daughters were attendees and I always brought my three-year-old daughter along when I was scheduled to teach. While driving there she asked, "Why are we going to Indian camp?"

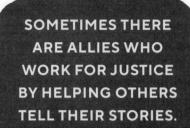

SOMETIMES THERE ARE ALLIES WHO WORK FOR JUSTICE BY HELPING OTHERS TELL THEIR STORIES.

"Well," I said, "you know we're Cherokee. Cherokee people are American Indians."

Her response was immediate and heartbreaking. "I don't want to be an Indian," she said. "Indians are ugly."

I didn't know what to say.

As a kid, I read books all the time. I wanted to read books about people who looked like me, but I couldn't find any. There were a lot of books that exploited "Native content," but by and large these books depicted Native people as either extinct, pan-Indigenous, or as stereotypes. Books like *Island of the Blue Dolphins* and *Little House on the Prairie* did real violence to the memories and histories of real Native people who were no longer living. The books from the big publishers tended to focus on a handful of tribes and were not created by Native writers. The main characters of many of the "Native books" were animals, literal animals. Nearly forty years later, the literary landscape had barely changed, with a few noteworthy and excellent exceptions.

However, it still shocked me that my child had internalized the belief that "Indians were ugly." How could this have happened? How had I failed so hard as a Cherokee parent?

My daughter's world was filled with positive images of Native Americans, including Cherokees. She loved her Cherokee relatives; my father, and her aunt and uncle, and her sisters.

She would never have called them "ugly." Using YouTube we watched Cherokee storytellers and she learned about our tribe from our tribe via OsiyoTV. I had taken her to visit the museums at Cherokee Nation and we went to see Native art wherever we could. I played recordings of Cherokee songs for her. Our walls were covered with art by Native American artists.

Yet, at three years old she was a sponge, and the powerful and negative images of Indians—or "Injuns" as they're called in the animated *Peter Pan*—had made an impression. The characters are painted bright red and have exaggerated features. They say "How" and "Ugh" and "Squaw" and they don't use contractions. "What makes the red man red?" they sang.

How do you protect a child from a world that has defined who they are for many, many years in negative and stereotypical ways?

HOW DO YOU PROTECT A CHILD FROM A WORLD THAT HAS DEFINED WHO THEY ARE FOR MANY, MANY YEARS IN NEGATIVE AND STEREOTYPICAL WAYS?

I was grateful that my young daughter was able to tell me what she believed. For her, I was able to try to course correct. Those movies are still out there, being remade and edited to be more palatable for a new generation. However, no amount of trigger warnings is going to undo the damage of racist images. I realized I had to be much more careful about the media my kids had access to. I had to counter all the bad with an exponential amount of good. But my children were not the only ones who needed good Native content by Native creators.

That day I realized that if I wanted these books, I might have to start writing them. I began to focus on creating stories that centered contemporary Native people. I thought a lot about what kind of books I wanted to put out into the world if I ever got a chance to be a published writer. I took classes on how to get published at the local community college. I worked on a middle grade mystery in my spare time. Eventually, a neighbor introduced me to a published author who was part of a small writing group. I was thrilled to be allowed to participate and get feedback on my completed manuscript.

In the critique group we exchanged chapters and the published white writer gave advice. She told me about her friends in the industry and the exclusive writing retreats she paid to attend. Her view of the publishing world was very competitive, and the more I learned about the inside track to getting published and financial costs for networking, the less optimistic I felt about my chances of success. She said if I wanted to get published I needed to go to the big writing conferences and network with people in the industry. From there, she suggested, I might be able to find an agent.

Conferences are not free and I wasn't making a lot of money at that time. Still, this was my dream. I budgeted the money for a big Texas writing conference, reserved a hotel room, and signed up for workshops. Once there, the published writer suggested we separate and network. In the big hotel ballroom I sat at a table with seven other excited would-be writers, but I didn't feel comfortable. This was not an intimate space. This was like the first day of school in a class of two hundred, and it seemed like most of the writers knew each other. The conference was largely attended by white people, panels were largely made up of white authors and illustrators, and all around me people struck up conversations with folks who looked like them. There were a few other non-white attendees, and they were a welcome sight, but there was only one other Native person there.

I had paid to learn how to become a published author and meet like-minded individuals. So, I tried, though I'm an introvert and this part of the writing business is hard for me. Many introverts would probably agree that when you already feel isolated, it gets harder, not easier to put yourself out there. Inevitably, exchanges with veritable strangers fell into a variety of microaggression categories. The dialogue, generally, went like this.

A soon as I take a bite of dry chicken, a stranger asks, "Do you speak your Native language?"

In my head I respond, "Do you, Ms.-Woman-with-great-grandparents-from- (insert European country here) speak your Native language? Would you if your father had been beaten for speaking it when he was a kid while trying to survive colonization?"

Me: "No."

Someone else would ask, "Do you practice your Native religion?"

Me in my head: And what do you think that would be, seeing as my father was sent to a boarding school run by Quakers and then attended a college set up by Methodist missionaries to the Cherokee?

Out loud I ask, "Which religion would that be?"

And, of course, the one question every Native person hears more often than not, "How much Indian are you?"

In my head: I was half, but you know, those darn mosquitoes.

I would generally respond in a way that confused most people,

HARVESTING THE STORIES OF OTHER
CULTURES, PARTICULARLY STEALING
STORIES FROM PEOPLE ONE'S ANCESTORS
HAVE ENSLAVED OR WHOSE ETHNIC
CLEANSING ONE'S ANCESTORS HAVE
BENEFITED FROM, IS A FORM OF
CONTINUED VIOLENT COLONIZATION. IT
OFTEN FEELS LIKE IT IS THE FINAL STEP IN
TRYING TO MAKE US DISAPPEAR.

"Cherokee Nation doesn't use Blood Quantum."

Often once non-Native people found out I was Cherokee
they wanted to know how they could prove they were Native
American, too. Unfortunately, many white writers seemed to
believe this would give them permission to tell the stories of
Native people, people whose homelands they had never visited,
people whose histories they didn't know, or whose historical
trauma they could only imagine. On the ride home, the
published white writer let me know in no uncertain terms
and at length that writers should be able to write whatever
story they want. I was trapped in a vehicle with her for hours.

"I think some stories should be told by people for whom it's
either their lived experience or the experience of their ancestors,
not simply imagined," I said a few times in as many different ways
as possible.

When a non-Native person tells me they have the right to tell
and sell Native stories I picture them metaphorically slipping
in and out of the skin of a Native person and I feel ill. Harvesting
the stories of other cultures, particularly stealing stories from

people one's ancestors have enslaved or whose ethnic cleansing one's ancestors have benefited from, is a form of continued violent colonization. It often feels like it is the final step in trying to make us disappear.

I came home disheartened once again. Living in Texas without a supportive writing community was lonely, and, in many ways, the conference left me feeling worse. I wondered if there was any space for me in publishing.

The published writer was right about one thing. No one becomes successful in publishing alone. Writers need allies. As a Native American writer, finding the right allies can be extra challenging for me and other marginalized authors. It was more difficult than just saving money to go to the big writing conferences or being in a critique group with published white writers.

I FELT WELCOME IN THIS SPACE THAT WAS CROWDED AND FILLED WITH THE JOYOUS VOICES OF PEOPLE I HAD YET TO MEET.

Were it not for my many allies, I would not be a published writer. Sometimes it's the editor who cheers you on or the agent who looks out for you and your stories. Sometimes it's the writing friend who recommends you for a project. Sometimes allies come in the form of a woman named Laura and a literary journal called *KWELI-Truth From the Diaspora's Boldest Voices*.

Laura Pegram is an artist, a writer, a jazz singer, an African American woman, and an ally. The words "Lifting while we climb" inform much of Laura's work and life and come from a National Association of Colored Women's Clubs slogan. She is the founding editor of *Kweli Journal* and one of the greatest models of allyship I know.

In an interview with Cherokee writer Traci Sorell for *Cynsations*, Cynthia Leitich Smith's blog, Laura said that while adjusting to a diagnosis of autoimmune disease she believed, for a time, that "the arts world . . . was now in my rearview mirror. Then one day I realized that it didn't have to be behind me; I could create an alternative arts community from my living room." Additionally, Laura saw how difficult it was for all marginalized writers and chose to lift while she, too, climbed. At a time when she was newly disabled and it would have been reasonable to focus on herself and her needs, Laura, once more, found a way to work for the good of the community.

In this way, *Kweli Journal* was created. *Kweli* means "truth" in Swahili, and their stated mission is to "nurture emerging BIPOC writers and create opportunities for their voices to be recognized and valued." The journal was a place where the truth could sing. *Kweli* also sponsored a children's literature conference. I applied for and received a scholarship that enabled me to attend.

The writing conference sponsored by *Kweli* was a completely different experience from all that had come before. The first time I met her in person, at the check-in tables for the Color of Children's Literature Conference, Laura's voice sang out to me, "Andrea, I'm so glad you're here!" The beautiful Manhattan building hummed with energy and I felt welcome in this space that was crowded and filled with the joyous voices of people I had yet to meet.

I was alone in New York City for the first time in my life, and at a writing conference created to support the needs of BIPOC writers and illustrators. I was surrounded by Brown faces and anticipated meeting other Native writers that morning. For an Indigenous writer accustomed to the microaggressions of majority white writing spaces, this was a new feeling.

Shirley Chisolm, the first Black woman elected to the US Congress said, "If they don't give you a seat at the table, bring a folding chair." BIPOC people have had to bring their own chairs to a lot of tables. As a Cherokee writer, even finding the tables in the publishing world had been a challenge. Laura Pegram saw a need for a table where marginalized writers could grow, a place where they could work on the stories singing in their souls. Laura Pegram built that table.

There were so many people whose voices needed to be amplified and Laura brought a microphone. Then Laura supplied chairs for Indigenous writers, too, at a conference that ended up being standing room only. Before I attended the *Kweli* conference, being a writer had been a lonely experience. For the first time, I felt like becoming a published author was truly in reach.

Kweli has impacted me and other Native writers in unforeseen and wonderful ways, including giving Native writers from all over the chance to connect and form writing groups and friendships. There was power in no longer being alone. *Kweli* gave us the space and the support to find and nurture a writing community where none had existed before.

Going back to New York City for *Kweli* in the spring is like going home. We hug, celebrate, and encourage each other.

No one makes it in publishing without allies. My story is no exception. When I got my first contract I cried. Because of all the women in my life, the Indigenous and Black women, particularly, I was going to get to tell a story of my tribe's experience that had previously been inaccurately and insufficiently told.

There are so many stories you have never heard. There are over 570 federally recognized tribes in these United States, all with stories of the impact of colonization and histories and cultures and languages of their own. We are still here. Yet, there is a huge absence of stories about us in today's world. Writers from our tribes are the ones whose voices the publishing industry should be amplifying.

Cornell West said, "Justice is what love looks like in public." Laura Pegram's work as an ally looks like love to me. Lifting while we climb is the fastest way to create the world I want to live in, the world I want to leave future generations.

I have no regrets about the conferences I went to, the ones where I felt like I was always holding my breath, waiting for the next microaggression. I learned a lot from many publishing experts.

And that one other Native writer I saw back in Texas wasn't an attendee. She was teaching and working to improve those spaces. *New York Times* best-selling writer and author-curator for publishing imprint Heartdrum, Cynthia Leitich Smith is a citizen of the Muscogee Nation. Later, when my first book was published, Cynthia used her voice to promote and celebrate it.

ALLYSHIP IS NOT FOR THE SELFISH.

To be cheered on by your literary heroes is no small thing. To be able to create the books your child needs in the world is a dream other people helped me make come true.

Allyship is not for the selfish. It might be showing up and speaking for someone who can't afford a fight with the establishment. It might be writing a check to support an emerging writer who just needs to go to that conference. An ally amplifies the voices of others, so we can all sing together. Laura Pegram has had to work constantly to make things better for herself, to move upward. But through *Kweli*, this jazz singer's allyship has done work that lifts up voices of marginalized writers that will sing on forever.

16

COUNTING ON ESTEBAN

MARIETTA B. ZACKER

"I'm not interested in allies who can go back into their privilege at any moment. I'm interested in accomplices who will stand alongside you when shit goes down." —Donja R. Love, Playwright, "40 Black playwrights on the theater industry's insidious racism," *Los Angeles Times,* October 2020

Sitting on the blue bench, I felt the presence of someone in front of me and heard, "What's your name?"

We were outside the main building. I sat as I always did, waiting for my older sister to come get me. Back on the first day at our new school, in a new place that wasn't home, she told me "nos encontramos en el banquillo azul." I had been doing that ever since.

Life is extra strange when you can't communicate with anyone. I sat on that blue bench and counted the pebbles underneath my feet as I moved them around, izquierda a derecha, left to right. The trail I made was still there from the day before, and the day before that. I was the only one who ever sat there it seemed. The path got deeper and more defined each day and it reminded me of the well-worn path underneath the swing where I played with my friends in Puerto Rico, except now it was just my lone foot making that indentation in the dirt. The memories kept me counting.

"What's your name?" I heard them ask again, louder this time. For the first time, I knew what they were asking. Maybe someone had asked me that before. It's hard to know when it's clear that people are speaking, yet you come up empty when those words reach your ears. I longed to hear the sounds I was accustomed to, en español, sounds that were as comfortable and familiar to me as the feeling of sand between my toes. Instead I saw mouths form into all sorts of shapes, then noises followed, but nothing intelligible. It had taken me days, maybe weeks, to figure out what I now understood to be "¿Cómo te llamas?" in English. Hearing this was like the sun rising to welcome me to the day. Except I wasn't at home on the island. Still, this was my opportunity to tell them that they should call me Marietta. It felt like an eternity, but regardless, I knew what it meant this time. Finally.

I counted the number of feet in front of me—uno, dos, tres, cuatro, cinco, seis. So there were three of them. My least favorite number in English.

As I looked at my clasped hands resting on my lap, I wondered who exactly I would encounter when I dared to raise my gaze. Would it be someone who typically smiled at me, someone who looked at me funny if our eyes ever locked for even a second, or someone who typically ignored me altogether? Every one of my classmates seemed to fall into one of those three categories. Hoping it was someone who belonged to the first group, I looked up with a slight grin. I recognized them, but their faces didn't show a smile. Their look was something different altogether—a mixture of curiosity and disgust. I felt like an unfamiliar animal they were seeing for the first time while on a visit to the zoo.

"Marietta," I said in the lowest voice possible, just audible enough for them to hear. I wouldn't give them more. I couldn't, even if I wanted to. I waited for them to speak again, hoping they would say something in Spanish—I was certain some of them at least spoke it—but I got nothing. They walked away laughing and

ANNOUNCING OUR
DEPARTURE TO OUR
FRIENDS IN ELEMENTARY
SCHOOL BEFORE WE
LEFT IN MID-DECEMBER
WAS LIKE PREPARING FOR A
HURRICANE, FEARING WHAT'S
TO COME WHILE KNOWING
THAT NO AMOUNT OF
PREPARATION CAN TRULY AND
FULLY PROTECT YOU.

peering at me and saying words I couldn't understand. I soon realized that was their point. Their laughter lasted in my head long after they were out of sight.

My foot swaying, I went back to counting. Counting kept me busy and counting distracted me from my reality. My family had decided to move to the United States in the middle of the school year. Announcing our departure to our friends in elementary school before we left in mid-December was like preparing for a hurricane, fearing what's to come while knowing that no amount of preparation can truly and fully protect you. As we said our last goodbyes, the wind picked up speed, then the storm arrived swiftly and forcefully when we boarded the plane to America. My tears rained onto my lap throughout the flight. Mami hoped that moving during the holiday break would give my sister and me enough time to adjust to the place we would now have to call home. Little did she know that those two weeks were simply the eye of the hurricane, with the storm gaining strength when she dropped us off at school for the first time.

I hung on to the blue bench, still hearing the laughter in my head, waiting for another set of strong winds to subside. Hurricane season seemed relentless that year. I counted with a vengeance, more than just the pebbles underneath my feet. I counted the people who tossed a ball back and forth. I counted steps as kids hopped. I counted the number of cars that passed. I counted the lines on my pleated skirt. I counted the screws on the blue bench. I counted time ticking away when there was nothing else left to count.

When we were in class, I felt safe, not because of the walls that protected me or the roof over my head, but because I knew I was supposed to be quiet when a teacher was present. This I had mastered. I sat silently and was grateful that numbers kept me company there as well, since whatever sounds I heard coming from the adult in the room were incomprehensible.

I could tell you how many of everything there was in every room I sat in. While the teacher spoke, I looked at the clock on the wall, watched the second hand tick, and waited patiently while the hands moved from five to ten to fifteen to twenty. Being quiet made things easier for me. The teacher must have been thrilled that I didn't disrupt her class and I was grateful not to be noticed. I followed along by copying whatever my classmates did. If they took out a book from underneath their desk, I did the same. I waited for them to open it, then I looked at the number on the corner of the page and turned to that. Numbers lending a lifeline again.

And on that blue bench, after finally being asked a question I understood, and for the first time being able to answer, no amount of counting helped. I was confused by the laughter. It was clear that they weren't pleased with my answer, but I simply didn't know why. Maybe I thought they were asking my name, but instead were asking something different. I couldn't be sure.

The English I was learning came mostly from *Sesame Street*. This was a show I should have long outgrown, but we moved to the United States without knowing any English, and my abuelos and Mami had no other way to help. So we all watched *Sesame Street* and tried to learn a different language together.

I was especially grateful for Count von Count. Numbers were familiar to me, so it made sense to me to learn how to say each one and practice speaking English this way. Abuelo and I would count out loud the pieces of the puzzle we were assembling, we would count out loud the number of times we stirred our scoops of ice cream to make our sopa de helado. Practicing how to say the numbers also helped me avoid other words that looked like gibberish on any page. Words were much more difficult because they made no sense. So I stuck with numbers, despite the number three giving me problems. Counting in Spanish, and then in English thanks to Count von Count, kept me occupied.

Yet I had to face my classmates daily and the numbers I could write and sort of speak were not enough to communicate with them.

Days after the name incident, and after figuring out how to push aside the laughter still stuck in my head, I felt someone sit down on the blue bench next to me for the first time. My foot stopped swaying. My eyes did not leave my lap. He said something that was indistinguishable to me, something in English, for sure. Yet the sounds were gentle—gentle enough for me to look at him sideways and shrug.

He must have sensed my fear at not knowing what he said, so he started again. "I'm Esteban," he said. "Marietta, right?" And he said my name the way Mami said it. And my abuelos. And my friends back home. It was as beautiful as the sound of the ocean waves on the shores in Puerto Rico.

My name was given to me to honor my grandfather, the light of my life. Our names shared the first four letters, and that always made me feel connected to him and special. Abuelo was my partner in all things, including sitting diligently alongside me, practicing his numbers the way Count von Count taught us.

AND HE SAID MY NAME THE WAY MAMI SAID IT. AND MY ABUELOS. AND MY FRIENDS BACK HOME. IT WAS AS BEAUTIFUL AS THE SOUND OF THE OCEAN WAVES ON THE SHORES IN PUERTO RICO.

Esteban didn't know, but saying my name as it was meant to be said, and not laughing, meant the world to me. Until that point, in my new school, in a different place from what I called home, where no one knew me, something about my name was wrong. It was strange to have to think about something that, up until now, was a given. My name was simply my name. Now people paused when they saw Marietta and stumbled while saying it. They twisted it and reshaped it and, many times, didn't even seem to try. Even roll call was an issue. I became a master at raising my hand if no one else did after hearing the "mmmm" sound. No one addressing me by name meant that I was always alone. Until Esteban.

"¿Esteban, tú hablas español?"

"Un poquito," he said, and he smiled. That was good enough for me. For the first time in a while, I didn't think about counting anything.

I don't remember how our friendship evolved next, but I do remember our walks. We strolled the fenced-in area close to the building, the blue bench always visible for when my sister arrived. Those walks were the only time when I felt that perhaps I could eventually find the calm after the storm, similar to the ocean resuming the regular ebb and flow of the tide after it's been forced to wreak havoc. It was a relief to be taking those steps with someone, even if few words were exchanged. During our silence, I counted our steps, but every day we spoke more and more.

In class, not much changed, except for Esteban, or Steve, as everyone but me seemed to call him. He smiled and waved as I walked in, which reminded me that after school he would say, "Hola, Marietta," bringing the soothing sounds of the sea back into my life. Watching Esteban a few rows up from me also gave me something else on which to focus. I counted the books he had underneath his desk. I counted the number of times he bounced his leg up and down. I counted the seconds it took for the teacher to call on him when he raised his hand. I counted the minutes left until I could walk with Esteban.

During one of our strolls, as we muddled through speaking Spanish, English, and I'm sure Spanglish, Esteban and I decided to exchange phone numbers. The very idea both thrilled me and scared me, but it was a good kind of scared. I had seen Count von Count count the number of times a phone rang, insisting he had to keep counting instead of letting Ernie answer the phone. When Esteban called me at home, I could picture myself counting the rings, but I would most certainly pick up the receiver before he had a chance to hang up. There was no Count to stop me, and having a friendship that extended beyond school meant hurricane season might be subsiding.

As Esteban asked me for my number, I knew this was my opportunity to bring to life what I had learned from Count von Count. I decided to say each digit in English rather than Spanish.

And as I did, Esteban and I both smiled at what we both knew was a feat. He had heard me say some words, but I was powering through only in English. Then I got to the fifth digit in my phone number and I paused. Esteban was smiling at me so I channeled Count von Count's energy and enthusiasm for numbers. "Three," I said.

The words from someone behind me felt like a strong gust, "It's three, not tree. You're in America now, you have to speak English, Mary." Then a forceful pull of my ponytail jerked my head backward, throwing me to the ground.

Esteban looked at me, his smile gone. My eyes went to his but I could not speak. Neither of us had the words. In any language.

"You're next, Steve," they told us as they walked away.

Esteban and I just stared at one another.

Then Esteban yelled, "It's Marietta, imbécil."

I was no longer in the safe neighborhood surrounding Sesame Street. Esteban and I were on our own. Perhaps we didn't have all the right words, but we had one another and that had to be enough. His forcefulness and fearlessness gave me courage to get up. Although I didn't have the words at my disposal, I held my head high and I felt ten feet tall. The kid turned and looked at us both as we stood side by side.

"Marietta y Esteban," Esteban continued. "That's what you can call us. Or don't call us anything at all."

Esteban took my hand and we walked away, leaving them speechless. Even if they had started yelling at us in English, for the first time, I didn't care. Strong winds continued to swirl, but I had someone by my side, anchoring me. Someone who cared

enough to call me by the only name I knew. Someone who saw me, who heard me, who allowed me to feel a warm calm breeze again, wrapping his arms around me like a tropical day on mi isla del encanto, no hurricane in sight.

Esteban and I stayed friends until high school, when my family moved to another part of town. He may go by Steve now, I don't know, but I am confident it's his choice rather than someone else's, and that makes a big difference. I am comforted by the memories of how he welcomed me and supported me—so much so that I eventually found my own voice, in both English and Spanish. I even got better at saying my numbers, although the three always makes me pause. I am grateful that I can now smile when I say it. I think of Esteban every time.

One thing held true during the time I knew him: Marietta and Esteban were the only names we let anyone call us. He eventually learned about Abuelo and our special bond, so when I faltered, he would remind me that Mami named me Marietta for a very good reason, and because of that, Abuelo would always be my side. Little did Esteban know that he would leave a similar lasting impression.

My name had a deep, intimate significance, so I cherished it; but it was also my identity, plain and simple, so it went beyond the personal when someone scoffed at it or laughed. I realized much later that pronouncing my name was only difficult because it was unfamiliar to people. It wasn't a hardship to say my name, it was simply different from what they knew, and that's what they didn't like. They were making the choice to knock me down, but their discomfort was on them. It was easier for people to be a gale force wind, wrecking without abandon. Being a calm, welcoming breeze required more thought and care. It was never about people saying my name perfectly—after all, I understood well that training your tongue to make new sounds was a feat—it was simply the desire for people to focus their warmth on a human interaction rather than choosing for it to power a storm.

As I found my voice, I realized how lucky I was that Esteban chose to sit on my blue bench. And although I kept watching *Sesame Street* with Abuelo for many years to come, I stopped relying on Count von Count and his numeric ways in order to escape and find my footing. As Abuelo and I gained more confidence in speaking a new language, Abuelo reminded me of my privilege in being able to move forward. He took me with him when he was helping someone navigate government forms or pay their bills by translating the paperwork, and he insisted we help the bodega owners even though their shop was far from where we lived.

IT WASN'T A HARDSHIP TO SAY MY NAME, IT WAS SIMPLY DIFFERENT FROM WHAT THEY KNEW, AND THAT'S WHAT THEY DIDN'T LIKE. THEY WERE MAKING THE CHOICE TO KNOCK ME DOWN, BUT THEIR DISCOMFORT WAS ON THEM.

My words come easier than they did back then, but I've never forgotten the instances which made me feel unseen and unwelcome. Today I fight for the voices not often heard in books, and it amazes me that so many years later, the battle Esteban fought for us, the one many fought before him, I am still fighting today. And when I hear people within publishing say that something that is unfamiliar to them will be too difficult for a reader to identify with, I feel the yank of the ponytail that snaps me back to that moment with Esteban, the moment that helped me see that the problem was their outlook, not my presence in our shared world.

I push back against people saying that a story does not belong or isn't important enough. I fight for the voices of those whose stories have been brushed aside for years, and I speak loudly when someone says that a reader will find something too difficult simply because it is unfamiliar.

It had been easy for Esteban to sit next to me and tell me he valued me by simply saying hello. The language of allyship is universal—it can be as easy as showing up. Yet it also means sticking around when the winds kick up, and holding fast when storms of dissent tell us our stories are unconventional and unwelcome. It is in those times that I think of the number three and move forward with conviction, forever indebted to Abuelo, Count von Count y Esteban.

TODAY I FIGHT FOR THE VOICES NOT OFTEN HEARD IN BOOKS, AND IT AMAZES ME THAT SO MANY YEARS LATER, THE BATTLE ESTEBAN FOUGHT FOR US, THE ONE MANY FOUGHT BEFORE HIM, I AM STILL FIGHTING TODAY.

STUFF TO THINK ABOUT, FURTHER READING, AND MORE RESOURCES

Hey, pals. It's Dana and Shakirah here, your stalwart co-editors.

Congratulations, you made it through this amazing collection! You're probably feeling tired, and a little bit overwhelmed, but that's okay. There's a lot to sort out, and a lot to think about. You might worry that you'll never learn everything, that there's too much to figure out, or that it's just too complicated. But take a breath. And again.

Remember: this isn't a race, or an exam where you're cramming for a final grade. All we can do is keep learning and trying.

The book might be over, but the conversation isn't done. There are lots of us doing this work, and lots of different resources—from websites to movies—to keep going. Below are just a few of the great books, websites, and organizations available, all recommended by the incredible authors in this book. There are hundreds more, and you may have suggestions as well, which is great! Keep a list, and be ready to share it when friends and family members are ready to join you on this path. Speaking of sharing, adults such as teachers, parents, and community mentors can help share the load if you need help researching or getting involved with organizations.

This list doesn't hold all the answers or promise to make you an expert, but it can offer you more stops along your journey. These resources can help you keep asking the right questions and build a community to seek out the answers.

Onward!

SOME GREAT ORGANIZATIONS

AIDA RECOMMENDS:

Bienestar is a long-standing organization that has helped with HIV testing and other support services to LGBTQIA+ community in Los Angeles.
www.bienestar.org

The Brown Boi Project focuses on changing the way communities of color talk about gender.
www.brownboiproject.org

A.J. RECOMMENDS:

Trans Lifeline is a peer support and crisis hotline 501 nonprofit organization serving transgender people by offering phone support and microgrants in the US and Canada. The resources page has sub-pages that provide comprehensive overviews on a variety of topics, such as coming out, non-binary and genderqueer identity, legal transition, social transition, etc.
www.translifeline.org/resources

ANDREA RECOMMENDS:

KWELI Journal An online magazine that empowers and nurtures up-and-coming writers of color.
www.kwelijournal.org

Cherokee Nation website All things Cherokee Nation, including incredible language resources.
www.cherokee.org

Official author site of **Cynthia Leitich Smith** and home of children's and YA lit resources, interviews, publishing insights, news, and more.
www.cynthialeitichsmith.com/cynsations

Official site of **The National Association of Colored Women's Clubs** Formed in the early 1900s, "Lifting As We Climb" is central to their mission and work.
www.nacwc.org

BRENDAN RECOMMENDS:

The People's Institute for Survival and Beyond has been offering powerful Undoing Racism® workshops and training sessions for over 40 years. The workshops provide analysis and an understanding for how racism manifests in people's lives and work, and they provide a framework for how to organize to Undo Racism in your community.
www.pisab.org

The Center for Racial Justice in Education's mission is to train and empower educators to dismantle patterns of racism and injustice in our schools and communities.
www.centerracialjustice.org

CAM RECOMMENDS:

Black Trans Femmes In the Arts is a community-based arts organization that builds community and mobilizes resources to support Black trans femme artists.
www.btfacollective.org

The LGBTQ+ Freedom Fund pays bail to secure the liberty and safety of low-income individuals in US jails and immigration facilities, with focus on LGBTQ+ individuals.
www.lgbtqfund.org

Brave Space Alliance is the first Black-led, trans-led, LGBTQ+ center located on the South Side of Chicago, dedicated to empowering and elevating queer and trans voices, particularly those belonging to people of color.
www.bravespacealliance.org

The Audre Lorde Project is a Lesbian, Gay, Bisexual, Two Spirit, Trans, and Gender Non-Conforming People of Color center for community organizing, focusing on the New York City area and dedicated to community wellness and progressive social and economic justice.
www.alp.org

DANA RECOMMENDS:

Facing History and Ourselves is an amazing organization that teaches social justice and the importance of being an "upstander" instead of a bystander, using history to challenge people to look at their behavior today.
www.facinghistory.org

The Youth Activism Project trains young people on how to take action in their communities and offers a bunch of tools to help train, engage, and amplify them.
www.youthactivismproject.org/activists-allies-community

Plan International is another youth activist organization that works globally, with a focus on gender equity and children's rights.
www.plan-international.org/youth-activism

Do Something is a youth-led group that helps young people connect to actions, causes, and activism.
www.dosomething.org/us

Hollaback! offers free online bystander intervention training programs, helping people know how to act quickly when they witness acts of harassment or violence.
www.ihollaback.org/bystanderintervention

DERICK RECOMMENDS:

National Stuttering Association provides support, friendship, and information to the stuttering community.
www.westutter.org

I.W. RECOMMENDS:

interACT: Advocates for Intersex Youth is the world's leading advocacy group for people with intersex traits, using a combination of media work, youth leadership development, and strategic litigation and legislative outreach to make the world a safer place for intersex people.
www.interactadvocates.org

InterConnect Support Group formerly known as the AIS-DSD Support Group, is a compassionate and affirming community of intersex individuals, family members, and allies, working together to promote a better quality of life through connection, support, education, and awareness.
www.interconnect.support

MARIETTA RECOMMENDS:

Learning for Justice is the education arm of The Southern Poverty Law Center, an incredible organization that fights white supremacy, racism, and systemic bias in the American South and beyond. There are tons of resources here for schools and communities, on subjects from race to immigration to bullying.
www.learningforjustice.org

SOME MORE GREAT ORGANIZATIONS

Anti-Bullying Alliance:
www.anti-bullyingalliance.org.uk

notOK app:
www.notokapp.com

Stonewall:
www.stonewall.org.uk

The Black Curriculum:
www.theblackcurriculum.com

The London Lesbian and Gay Switchboard:
www.switchboard.lgbt

The Trevor Project:
www.thetrevorproject.org

UK National Bullying Helpline:
www.nationalbullyinghelpline.co.uk

SOME GREAT BOOKS

A.J. RECOMMENDS:

The Trevor Project's Coming Out Handbook
**www.thetrevorproject.org/wp-content/uploads/2019/10/
Coming-Out-Handbook.pdf**

DANA RECOMMENDS:

So You Want to Talk About Race by Ijeoma Oluo

How to Be an Antiracist by Ibram X. Kendi

A People's History of the United States by Howard Zinn

Why Are All the Black Kids Sitting Together in the Cafeteria?
by Beverly Daniel Tatum

March Trilogy (graphic novels) by John Lewis, Andrew Aydin,
and Nate Powell

When They Call You a Terrorist: A Black Lives Matter Memoir
by Patrisse Khan-Cullors and asha bandele

Good Talk by Mira Jacob

How We Fight For Our Lives by Saeed Jones

Beyond Magenta: Transgender Teens Speak Out by Susan Kuklin

A Queer History of the United States by Michael Bronski and
Richie Chevat

*She/He/Me/They: For the Sisters, Misters, and Nonbinary
Resisters* by Robyn Ryle

ERIC RECOMMENDS:
Fiction
See No Color by Shannon Gibney

Nonfiction
All You Can Ever Know by Nicole Chung

I.W. RECOMMENDS:

#OwnVoices Intersex Books:

Fiction

A Proper Young Lady by Lianne Simon

Just Ash by Sol Santana

Nonfiction

Born Both by Hida Viloria

Contesting Intersex: The Dubious Diagnosis by Georgiann Davis

Raising Rosie by Eric and Stephani Lohman

XOXY by Kimberly Zieselman

LIZZIE RECOMMENDS:

Disability Visibility: First-Person Stories From the Twenty-First Century, edited by Alice Wong

SHAKIRAH RECOMMENDS:

Fiction

New Kid by Jerry Craft

Two Sisters: A Story of Freedom by Kereen Getten

Windrush Child by Benjamin Zephaniah

Nonfiction

Black and British: A Short, Essential History by David Olusoga

Stamped: Racism, Antiracism, and You: A Remix by Ibram X. Kendi & Jason Reynolds

This Book is Anti-Racist: 20 Lessons On How to Wake Up, Take Action, and Do the Work by Tiffany Jewell and Aurelia Durand

SHARAN RECOMMENDS:

Why I'm No Longer Talking to White People About Race by Reni Eddo-Lodge

SOME GREAT WEBSITES

A.J. RECOMMENDS:

LGBTQReads blog by Dahlia Adler
www.lgbtqreads.com

The Trevor Project's Guide to Being an Ally to Transgender and Nonbinary Youth
www.thetrevorproject.org/resources/ trevor-support-center/a-guide-to-being-an-ally-to-transgender- and-nonbinary-youth

DANA RECOMMENDS:

Sites to find diverse books by diverse authors:

Asian Author Alliance
www.asianauthoralliance.com

Diverse Bookfinder
www.diversebookfinder.org

Latinxs in Kid Lit
www.latinosinkidlit.com

Social Justice Books
www.socialjusticebooks.org

The Brown Bookshelf
www.thebrownbookshelf.com

We Need Diverse Books
www.diversebooks.org

YA Pride
www.yapride.org

KAYLA RECOMMENDS:

Alice Wong's Disability Visibility Project
www.disabilityvisibilityproject.com

Disability in Kidlit
www.disabilityinkidlit.com

SHAKIRAH RECOMMENDS:

Autistic Hoya
www.autistichoya.com/p/ableist-words-and-terms-to-avoid.html

Resources for traveling while black:

Black and Abroad
www.weareblackandabroad.com

Oneika the Traveller
www.oneikathetraveller.com/category/travelling-while-black

SHARAN RECOMMENDS:

Burnt Roti
www.burntroti.com

SOME GREAT DIGITAL MEDIA

ANDREA RECOMMENDS:

Osiyo, Voices of the Cherokee People, an Emmy Award–winning series about Cherokee people, history, and culture. *www.osiyo.tv*

DERICK RECOMMENDS:

Jacquelyn Joyce on YouTube

SHARAN RECOMMENDS:

Mississippi Masala (Rated R), a film directed by Mira Nair

Code Switch, a podcast from NPR

SOME MORE GREAT DIGITAL MEDIA

PODCASTS:

Do the Work, hosted by Brandon Kyle Goodman

Pod Save the People, hosted by DeRay Mckesson

The Alphabet Mafia Podcast, hosted by Ryan Zanardi

The Guilty Feminist, hosted by Deborah Frances-White

What the Trans!?, hosted by Michelle Snow and Ashleigh Talbot

Yo, Is This Racist?, hosted by Andrew Ti

SOCIAL MEDIA ACCOUNTS:

@ckyourprivilege (Instagram)

@Disabilityreframed (Instagram)

@everydayracism_ (Instagram)

@theconsciouskid (Instagram)

NATALIE AND NAOMI OFFER SOME GREAT ANTI-RACISM ADVICE

Natalie and Naomi Evans are the founders of Everyday Racism, a platform dedicated to sharing anti-racism resources and testimonies from BIPOC. Be a part of the anti-racism movement on Instagram @everydayracism_

HOW TO AVOID THE BYSTANDER EFFECT

What contributes to the bystander effect?

▶ Conscious and unconscious bias

▶ Being fearful

▶ Believing it's not your responsibility

▶ Thinking someone else will step in

▶ Remaining unaware

▶ Prejudice and discrimination

HOW TO BECOME AN ACTIVE BYSTANDER

▶ Learn how to become a better ally: read, listen to podcasts, and watch programs.

▶ Address your conscious and unconscious bias.

▶ Learn the language to interrupt the situation and educate yourself.

▶ Remind yourself that this is your responsibility.

▶ Remember, when you intervene it can also encourage others to step up.

WAYS TO CALL OUT RACISM

The more you learn about being anti-racist and being an anti-racist ally, the more difficult conversations you will have with friends, family, and other people around you.

If you struggle with any form of confrontation, then learn these basic responses to help you. Keep educating yourself. You may not always change someone's perspective in that moment and that's okay. It can take time. Reflect on whether the most effective way of having these conversations is publicly or privately, and ensure that it's safe to do so. Remember it's important to communicate when you don't agree, otherwise people may assume you are aligned with their racist comments.

Here are some useful phrases to use when you encounter racist comments:

▶ "Before you carry on, I would just like to address what you said about ____. That is something I find very offensive because ____ and I would like it if you didn't say that anymore."

▶ "Would you mind explaining what you mean by that? I would be interested to know where you got that information from."

▶ "What you just said made me feel uncomfortable because ____ and I would appreciate if you didn't say that again."

▶ "I/we am/are learning how to be actively anti-racist and I/we have realized that saying ____ is not ok. I/we would suggest reading/following ____."

▶ "You may or may not have meant to come across this way but saying ____ is actually very insulting."

▶ "I'd be really interested in chatting with you more about this at some point because I think there is more to unpack here."

SELF REFLECTION PROMPTS

Throughout this book you've been asked to read other people's words, and imagine yourself in other people's shoes. Empathy is a critical part of being an ally: we all have to learn how to step outside ourselves and recognize that other folks' lived reality might be very different from our own.

At the same time, we also need to turn our focus inward and process all this complicated stuff! How does reading this make you feel? How can reflecting on our past assumptions, choices, and actions help us make different choices in the future?

You might want to start a journal, a place to gather your thoughts and process things as you explore different ways of being an ally. There is no wrong way to do it! Whether you record voice notes on your phone, use a fancy notebook, or jot things down on paper napkins and save them in a box . . . just find a way of exploring your thoughts and keep track of your journey. (Just use clean napkins because . . . gross.)

Below are a few ideas to get you started, but don't stop here! Keep thinking, keep reflecting, keep trying . . . you got this.

xoxo Shakirah and Dana

1. Can you think of five ways to greet a group of people that doesn't reference gender? What could that sound like?

2. Write about a time you witnessed an act of casual racism. Did other people notice? How did the individual who experienced the act react? How did you react? What might you do differently next time?

3. Have you ever experienced somebody acting as an "upstander," where they disrupted an act of racism or other systemic bullying? How did they do it? What did they say or do? Do you think you could do something like that? Why or why not?

4. Picture a place you go frequently—school, an arcade, a store . . . anywhere! Now think about how accessible it is. Are there stairs to the entrance? Is there a ramp? How wide are the aisles? Could a wheelchair fit? How high are the counters? What does this show you about how disabled folks might be excluded from different public spaces?

5. Lizzie advised that you train yourself against making assumptions about disabled people, but you can interrogate your brain for judgmental thoughts against all marginalized persons. Think about a time you made a quick assumption. Ask yourself where you learned this information. Was it from TV or a movie? What do people from the marginalized group have to say about it? Do you need to go learn more?

SOME GREAT WORD SWAPS

Remember that old saying, "Sticks and stones may break my bones, but words will never hurt me?" Yeah, that's not really true though, is it? Words are powerful, and truthfully, they can cause pain—sometimes lots of it. Brendan says "language matters," and he's totally right. There are some words that seem harmless—you might use them every day and not even realize it—but some of these terms can actually make people feel pretty bad about themselves.

You can be an ally by paying attention to the words you choose. It takes practice to break old habits, so don't worry if you don't always get it right. The important thing is to try your best to make little, but powerful changes. Are there any other words or phrases you can think of that you could swap out?

Instead of this → **Try this**

Are you deaf? → **Are you listening?**

That's crazy! → **That's wild!**

This is lame. → **This is uncool.**

You're so OCD. → **You're so well-organized.**

This is retarded. → **This is silly.**

That's gay! → **That's boring!**

I feel seen/heard. → **I feel like you understand me.**

ABOUT THE AUTHORS

Shakirah Bourne (she/her) is a Barbadian author and filmmaker whose work has won numerous awards. She's known for her use of dialect and how she explores local culture, often exposing hypocrisy, and revealing hidden aspects of a so-called Caribbean paradise. Recently, she has been writing for young people who like mythological and fantastical tales, beginning with her debut children's novel, *Josephine Against the Sea*. Find her online @shakirahwrites or www.shakirahbourne.com.

Derick Brooks (he/him) is a Virginia-based author and illustrator who loves to create adventurous stories about people of color. He is the illustrator of *Bright Family* (Epic) and Lamar Giles' *The Last Chance for Logan County* (HMH 2021.) He is slated to contribute to Dapo Adeola's collaborative picture book *Hey You!* (Puffin 2021) and is also hard at work on his debut graphic novel *Grip Up!* about an interplanetary thumb wrestling camp for kids (Iron Circus 2022.) He is married to Dr. Lauren D. Kendall Brooks, a brilliant Black woman who stutters, and is glad to continue the conversation on how to be a stuttering ally and stand in solidarity with persons who stutter.

Sharan Dhaliwal founded and runs the UK's leading South Asian magazine *Burnt Roti*—a platform for young creatives to showcase their talent, find safe spaces, and destigmatize topics around mental health and sexuality, amongst others. She is the Director of Middlesex Pride and creator of Oh Queer Cupid, a queer speed dating and comedy night. She has had bylines in *i-D, HuffPost,* and the *Guardian,* and listed as a global influential woman for BBC 100 Women in 2019. Sharan has continued conversations around anti-Blackness in South Asian communities, with the release of the latest issue of *Burnt Roti* in December 2020.

Naomi Evans (she/her) is a 37-year-old teacher, writer, speaker, and anti-racist educator. She is married, and mother of two young children. She has experienced racism both overtly and covertly throughout her life and is passionate about seeing changes in the education system so that all students' experiences are represented. She cofounded @everydayracism_ with her sister, Natalie, and creates material to help support people to be actively be anti-racist in their everyday life.

Natalie Evans (she/her) is a 30-year-old event manager, writer, and anti-racism educator from Kent. Natalie is of Black Jamaican and White British heritage and grew up in a white majority town before moving to Brighton. She has recently moved back to her hometown and reflected on the racism she has experienced and how to educate others about being an ally. She cofounded @everydayracism_, an educational platform that amplifies the voices of BIPOC, in May 2020 after a video of her confronting two men racially abusing a ticket conductor went viral on Twitter.

I.W. Gregorio is a practicing urologist by day, masked avenging YA writer by night. She is the author of the Schneider Award-winning *This Is My Brain in Love*, and the Lambda Literary Finalist *None of the Above*. As an ally, she is proud to be a board member of interACT: Advocates for Intersex Youth, and is a founding member of We Need Diverse Books. Her essays have appeared in the anthologies *Hope Nation*, *Body Talk*, and *Our Voices, Our Stories*. Find her online at www.iwgregorio.com and on Twitter/Instagram at @iwgregorio.

Lizzie Huxley-Jones is an autistic author and editor based in London. They are the editor of *Stim*, an anthology of autistic authors and artists, which was published by Unbound in April 2020 to coincide with World Autism Awareness Week, and they work with authors and editors on sensitive portrayals of autistic characters. They are also the author of the children's biography *Sir David Attenborough: A Life Story*, and an editor at independent micropublisher 3 of Cups Press. They tweet too much at @littlehux, taking breaks to walk their dog Nerys.

Adiba Jaigirdar was born in Dhaka, Bangladesh, and has been living in Dublin, Ireland, since the age of 10. She has a BA in English and History from University College Dublin, and an MA in Postcolonial Studies from the University of Kent. Her studies have spanned critical theory which helped shape her work as both an ally and an author. She's the author of *The Henna Wars* and *Hani and Ishu's Guide to Fake Dating*. All of her work is aided by many cups of tea and a healthy dose of Janelle Monáe and Hayley Kiyoko. When not writing, she enjoys reading, playing video games, and ranting about the ills of colonialism.

Brendan Kiely is *The New York Times* bestselling author (with Jason Reynolds) of *All American Boys* and other novels, and a work of nonfiction, *The Other Talk: Reckoning With Our White Privilege*. As a frequent public speaker in schools across the country, he promotes allyship through an honest look at privilege, power, and accountability.

Dana Alison Levy (she/her) is an American author of many acclaimed books for young readers, including *It Wasn't Me* and the Family Fletcher novels. Her first novel for teens, *Above All Else*, was published in 2020. When not writing, Dana enjoys traveling, eating, taking photos of her cats, and smashing toxic white supremacist patriarchal norms. She makes a lot of mistakes and tries to learn from them. Find her at www.danaalisonlevy.com or wasting time on Twitter or Instagram @danaalisonlevy.

Cam Montgomery (enby she/her) resides in Seattle where she writes Young Adult novels (*Home and Away* and *By Any Means Necessary* are available now!). Currently, she finds herself the editor of an anthology titled *All Signs Point to Yes* (to be published in winter of 2022!). By day, Cam writes about Black teens across all their intersections. By night, she tends bar and binges Netflix. Cam has been out as queer since 2011, but lived quietly in it for years before that. In a decade of being Black *and* Out™, Cam has grown into the sunflower she was meant to be, with the support of fellow LGBTQ+ flowers.

Andrea L. Rogers is a citizen of the Cherokee Nation. She grew up in Tulsa, Oklahoma, but currently splits time between Fort Worth, Texas, and the University of Arkansas in Fayetteville. She graduated with an MFA from the Institute for American Indian Arts. Her literary horror and speculative fiction stories have been published in *Waxwing*, *Yellow Medicine Review*, *The Santa Fe Literary Review*, *Transmotion*, *The Massachusetts Review*, and *River Styx*. Capstone published her children's book *Mary and the Trail of Tears* which was included on the best books of 2020 by both NPR and American Indians in Children's Literature. Her essay, "My Oklahoma History" appeared in *You Too? 25 Voices Share Their #METoo Stories* from Inkyard Press. Her short story "The Ballad of Maggie Wilson" is included in *Ancestor Approved: Intertribal Stories for Kids*, a MG short story anthology from Heartdrum, an imprint of HarperCollins. Her next book is a picture book called *When We Gather*. It will be published by Heartdrum.

Aida Salazar is an award-winning author, translator, and arts activist whose writings for adults and children explore issues of identity and social justice. She is the author of the critically acclaimed middle grade verse novels, *The Moon Within* (International Latino Book Award Winner) and *Land of the Cranes* (California Library Association Beatty Award, Charlotte Huck Award Honor, Jane Addams Peace Honor). Her forthcoming books include *In the Spirit of a Dream: 13 Stories of Immigrants of Color*, *Jovita Wore Pants: The Story of a Revolutionary Fighter*, *A Seed in the Sun*, and the anthology *The Gift: Period Stories by MG Authors of Color*. Aida is a founding member of both LAS MUSAS—a Latinx kidlit author collective and LATINX LUNA—a collective challenging period stigmas in Latinx communities. She lives with her family of artists in a teal house in Oakland, California.

A.J. Sass (he/they) is an author, editor, and competitive figure skater who is interested in how intersections of identity, neurodiversity, and allyship can impact story narratives. He is the author of *Ana on the Edge* and *Ellen Outside the Lines* (Little, Brown), as well as a contributor to the *This Is Our Rainbow: 16 Stories of Her, Him, Them, and Us* anthology (Knopf). He currently lives in the San Francisco Bay Area with his boyfriend, a handful of aquarium fish, and two cats who act like dogs. Visit him online at sassinsf.com or @matokah on Twitter and Instagram.

Eric Smith is a literary agent and author from Elizabeth, New Jersey. He's worked on award-winning and *New York Times* bestselling books. As an author, his books include *The Girl and the Grove*, *Don't Read the Comments*, *You Can Go Your Own Way*, and the anthology *Battle of the Bands*, co-edited with Lauren Gibaldi. Both as an author and a publishing professional, he strives to get diverse and inclusive worlds onto bookshelves. He lives in Philadelphia with his wife and son.

Kayla Whaley lives outside Atlanta where she buys too many books and drinks too many lattes. Her work has appeared in the anthologies *Here We Are: Feminism for the Real World*, *Unbroken*, and *Vampires Never Get Old*, as well as in publications like *Bustle*, *Catapult*, and *Michigan Quarterly Review*. She holds an MFA in creative nonfiction from the University of Tampa and was senior editor at Disability in Kidlit.

Marietta B. Zacker (she/her) fights for words daily, words that eluded her when she moved to the United States from Puerto Rico. As a literary agent, she champions the work of authors and illustrators, helping these artists communicate their stories. Connecting with others and helping them find their voices is a key part of Marietta's everyday life. Alongside her soulmate, she is resolute in raising three thoughtful, strong human beings in her home away from home in New Jersey. You can find her online at www.mariettabzacker.com.

ACKNOWLEDGMENTS

SHAKIRAH:
We couldn't have done this project without Super-Agent Marietta B. Zacker, who brought us together, and advised, guided, commiserated, and ultimately added her own amazing words.

DANA:
And big thanks to the entire DK team, especially Tori Kosara, who juggled a million flaming chainsaws, and Anne Sharples, and the rest of the super-talented art, editorial, and marketing teams.

SHAKIRAH:
And don't forget fairies like Ayesha Gibson-Gill, Lisa Stringfellow, Lisa Springer, and Lloyda Garrett. Thank you to all of our family and friends who supported us with words of encouragement and advice. We love you!

DANA:
And most importantly, this project would never exist without the incredible talent and grace of the authors who trusted us with their stories. Thank you for your patience with us as we learned to be editors.

SHAKIRAH:
And cake. We can't forget cake and all your cats.

DANA:
And a final heartfelt thanks to Shakirah, my sister-from-another-mister, without whom I would have given up on this project and run into the sea months ago.

SHAKIRAH:
#DakirahForever

DK | Penguin
Random
House

Senior Editor Tori Kosara
Editorial Assistant Nicole Reynolds
Senior Art Editor Anne Sharples
Designer Anita Mangan
Production Editor Siu Yin Chan
Senior Production Controller Louise Minihane
Managing Editor Paula Regan
Managing Art Editor Jo Connor
Publishing Director Mark Searle

DK would like to thank the editors, Shakirah Bourne
and Dana Alison Levy; the authors; Marietta B. Zacker
at Gallt & Zacker Literary Agency; Caroline Richmond
and the team at We Need Diverse Books; and Bianca
Hezekiah for authenticity review. Also, at DK, Megan
Douglass for proofreading; Anne Damerell, Nicola Evans,
Emily Kimball, Grace Nyaboko, and Nishani Reed;
Ruth Amos for editorial help; and the DK Diversity,
Equity & Inclusion team, in particular the Product
and Content Working Group and Lisa Gillespie for
their insight and guidance.